EXTREME ORIGAMI

WON PARK

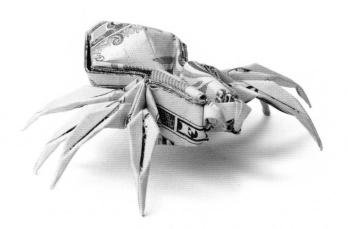

Race Point
PUBLISHING

Race Point
PUBLISHING

A division of Book Sales, Inc.
276 Fifth Avenue Suite 206
New York, New York 10001

RACE POINT PUBLISHING and the distinctive Race Point Publishing logo
are trademarks of Book Sales, Inc.

© 2012 by The Book Shop, Ltd.
7 Peter Cooper Road
New York, NY 10010

This 2012 edition published by Race Point Publishing by arrangement with
The Book Shop, Ltd.

Instructions and diagrams: Marcio Noguchi
Editor: Sherry Gerstein
Design: Tim Palin Creative
Photography: Joshua Griffler Photography

ISBN-13: 978-1-937994-02-0

Printed in China

4 6 8 10 9 7 5 3

www.racepointpub.com

To my first teacher—my mother—and to Tiffany, who inspires me.

CONTENTS

6 INTRODUCTION

8 TERMS AND SYMBOLS

10 ARE YOU READY TO TAKE THE *EXTREME ORIGAMI* CHALLENGE?

12 BUTTERFLY

16 TOILET

22 TANK

28 SPIDER

32 FOX

36 PIG

42 SWORDFISH

48 SEA TURTLE

52 OX

58 PEGASUS

64 PRAYING MANTIS

70 STAG BEETLE

76 CAR

84 FIGHTER JET

92 BAT

100 SCORPION

106 KOI FISH

114 STEGOSAUR

120 DRAGON

132 FORMULA 1 RACE CAR

143 ACKNOWLEDGMENTS

144 ABOUT THE AUTHOR

INTRODUCTION

Won Park's highly creative and intricate work has long been admired throughout the origami community. His dollar bill designs are some of the most challenging and popular, and there are legions of people around the world who fold nothing but paper money. Despite the popularity of the form, only a relatively small number of talented, creative artists publish money folds, and Won Park is widely regarded as a leading master of this specialty.

The US dollar bill is a popular format because it is readily available and relatively affordable, it is rich with intricate and artful engravings, and it is permanently printed on wonderfully strong, crisp stock. This medium stands up well to heavy folding and is particularly suited to wet-folding and the artful shaping that wet-folding affords. The dollar bill's rich tapestry of whorls, leaves, letters, and even an eye, are all elements that can be incorporated into the design of the money fold.

Since the rectangular proportions of US paper currency are fixed despite denomination, every design can be folded with a bill of any value. Fresh paper currency is strong and archival. It will not easily tear when folded, nor crumble with age, so it should last for generations. When you present a gift of cleverly folded cash, expect surprise and delight! It is sad indeed that so many countries are in the process of replacing their smaller paper denominations with coins.

Won's attention to detail is remarkable, but that is not unusual for an origami designer of this caliber. What is unusual is the combination of his eye for detail, his meticulous folding execution, and his finely tuned sense of artistry. Some time ago, when we were setting up our Origami Dō show in Waikiki, Hawaii—a short drive from Won's house—we received a dollar as change from a local grocery clerk. It felt curiously soft, and upon closer examination, we noticed it had been divided by dozens of crossing creases. We kept the bill safe until the next time we saw Won. We showed it to him and asked, "Do you recognize this?"

"Where did you get it? This is my koi!" was Won's reply. He explained that once in a while he would unfold a bill and use it as spending money if the folding wasn't proceeding to his liking.

We appreciate Won's intricate designs even more when they are folded from larger rectangles of handmade papers, such as the papers that we make here at Origamidō Studio. Won folded a larger version of his Koi from this special, handmade paper, and we proudly displayed it to an enthusiastic response from the public.

Won is also generous with his time. He taught at our studio during the show in Waikiki as well as at the local libraries around Oahu, and for Scott Macri's ongoing Hawaii Origami Club workshops. Won has been and continues to be an honored guest at many origami conventions and gatherings around the world.

We know that this eagerly anticipated title would not have been possible without the hard work of his illustrator, Marcio Noguchi—another generous, dedicated, and talented origami artist. Marcio's careful attention to detail and his eye for the flow of the folding sequence are evident in these clear, concise, and accessible diagrams.

We look forward to more of Won's amazing designs being published, and to the ongoing floodgate of new designs by his growing number of protégés.

Michael LaFosse and Richard Alexander
Origamidō Studio

TERMS AND SYMBOLS

— — — — — —   Valley fold

—·—·—·—·—··   Mountain fold

————————   Existing crease

····················   Hidden lines

 Preliminary fold

 Petal fold

 Rabbit-ear fold

 Swivel fold

 Squash fold

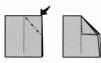 Inside reverse fold

 Outside reverse fold

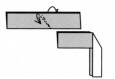 Closed sink

 Open Sink

 Spread sink

Pleat fold

Crimp fold

Waterbomb base

Bird base

(a)   (b)

(c)   (d)   (e)

Fold

Fold and unfold

Repeat

Open layers

Push/apply pressure

Rotate

Turn over

Close up

View from this angle

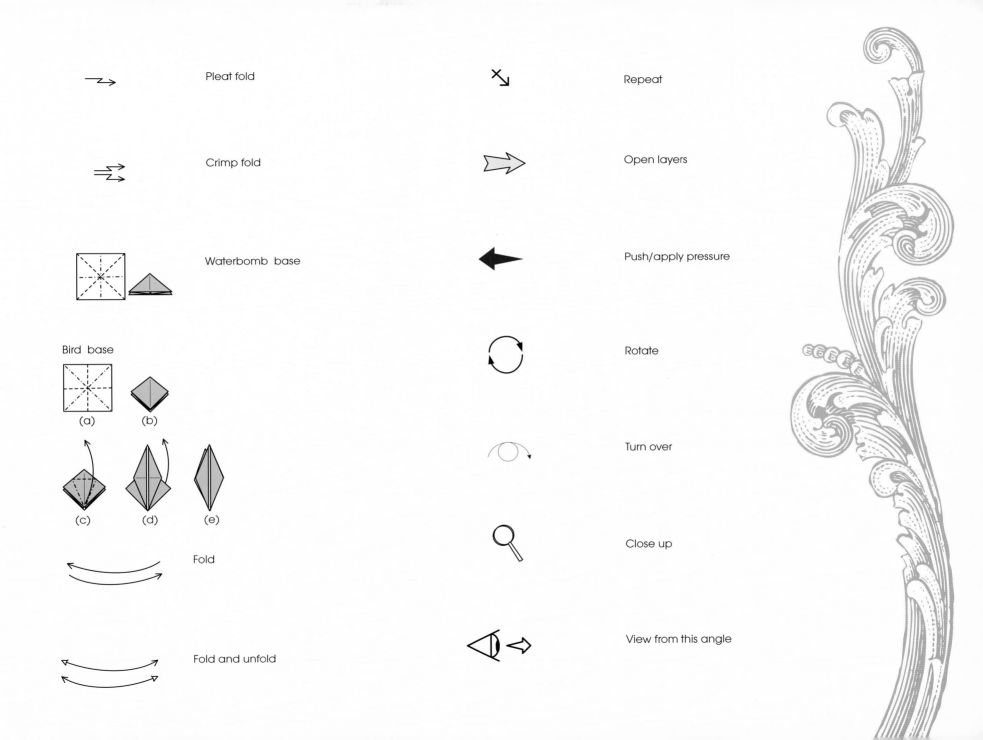

ARE YOU READY TO TAKE THE
EXTREME ORIGAMI CHALLENGE?

As with anything you do, origami—especially extreme origami—takes practice. Lots of practice. If you are already an advanced folder, you are well prepared to take the *Extreme Origami* challenge offered by this book. But if your skills are at an intermediate level, here are some tips that will help you attack these models.

- Origami instructions can be tricky to follow. Most of the action is shown in the diagrams, but the text is important, too. Learn to read both together to get the whole story.

- Some important folds are referred to by name; they are listed in the terms section. Read the terms through and learn them before you start these models.

- Equip yourself with these basic tools when you are ready to begin folding:

  (1) Practice paper—use plain papers that are larger than (but with the same proportions as) regular dollar bills, if you can. They will make the tiniest folds a little easier to learn. You will need to practice these models a lot before using real money to fold them. One of the challenges of folding with real money is that it has patterns and artwork printed on it that can make it hard to see the creases. So the value of getting up to speed on plain practice paper can't be oversold.

  (2) A bone folder, for making sharp, accurate folds. Imprecise folds can throw the whole model off.

  (3) Tweezers, for grasping small folds firmly. It takes a bit of practice to learn how to use them properly.

  (4) Small paper clamps, for helping thickly folded paper to keep its shape.

  (5) Fresh, new dollar bills, for when you are ready to fold tight, crisp final models.

- When folding, compare the current step to the results in the step ahead. Sometimes knowing what the final result should look like will enable you to execute a particularly difficult step.

- Beware of overfolding. Paper softens with use—even durable stock like dollar bills—and when it is too soft, the folds won't hold. Which is yet another good reason to practice, practice, practice.

- Sometimes you just need to step away from your project. These projects are extremely challenging. There will be times when you will throw your hands up in frustration. That's when it is time to take a break and a breather. A little perspective always helps.

- Enjoy the process. Stay focused on making sharp, accurate folds and the rest will follow with time and practice.

- Allow yourself time to fold these models. They are works of art; making art takes time. Final shaping details are as important to the end product as the intermediate steps, so give these your full attention, too.

1 Fold in half horizontally and vertically. Unfold.

2 Fold the edges along the short vertical crease.

3 Turn over.

4 Fold the angle bisectors, crease to crease and edge to crease.

5 Fold existing mountain creases to the center crease.

6 Turn over.

7 Inside reverse fold, using existing creases.

8 Turn over.

9 Rabbit-ear fold, using existing creases. The top will not lie flat.

10 Push the layers inside into a kind of inside reverse, so that everything will lie flat. Repeat on the other side.

(In progress)

11 Pinch to create reference points. First, bring the edge to the crease, then the pinch to the crease, and finally the last pinch to the crease. Repeat on the other side

12 Swivel fold: first, create a valley fold starting at the ⅛ mark and bring the mountain crease to close to the ¼ pinch. Fold the top edge down a tiny bit, creasing so that everything lies flat.

(View from back)

13 Repeat on the other side.

14 Wrap around (outside reverse).

15 Turn over. Detailed view of wings is next.

16 Valley fold the corner in, then fold the top layer up, finessing as needed so paper lies flat. Repeat on other side.

17 Lift the flap, slightly marking existing crease.

18 Pre-crease: fold the center crease into a folded edge and bring to the corners, pivoting from the intersection of the creases.

19 Reverse the creases from valley to mountain; valley fold the center crease.

20 Crease the angle bisectors.

21 Mountain crease the angle bisectors.

22 Start the collapse: push the head part down, and bring the edges together. The model will not lie flat.

23 Collapse the tail along existing creases and fold in half while folding the wings down to meet.

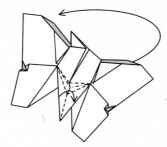

24 Valley fold the wings from the pivot point along the dashed line. They will close on the other side, while the tail will swivel down.

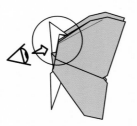

25 View from the top for details of the head.

BUTTERFLY

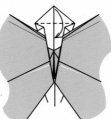

26 Open slightly. Valley fold the inside tip of the head from corner to corner.

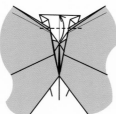

27 Fold the tip back to the edge. Close.

28 View from the inside for more head detail. Open the wings.

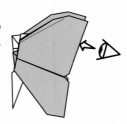

29 Move the flap to the center to allow space to fold the edge to edge. Move the flap back, and fold the corner to the center line. Repeat on the other side.

30 View from the top again to adjust wings. Press wings out to open them up.

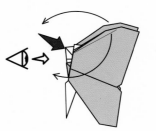

The completed butterfly

TOILET

Precision folds are very important with this model.

1 Fold in half. Unfold.

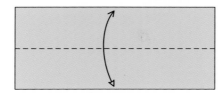

2 Fold edges to crease and unfold. Turn over.

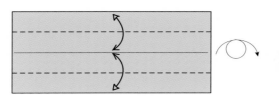

3 Fold edges to the creases indicated and unfold. Turn over.

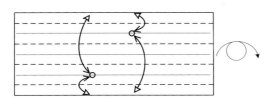

4 Fold the short edge to the long edges and unfold to crease the angle bisectors.

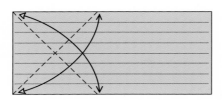

5 Crease at the points indicated.

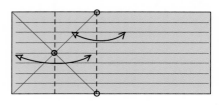

6 Fold to the crease and unfold. Turn over.

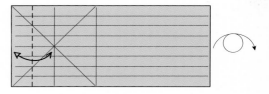

7 Crease in half.

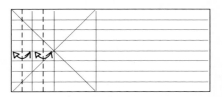

8 Fold edge to the crease. Unfold. Turn over.

9 Pinch the edges between the creases.

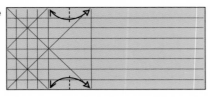

10 Fold the crease to the pinches created in the last step. Unfold.

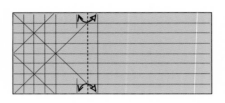

11 Crease between the edge and the pinches as well as between the creases shown.

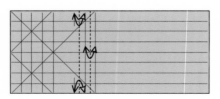

12 Valley fold.

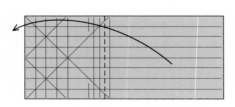

13 Create symmetrical creases using the creases on the layer beneath as reference.

Use crease from layer beneath for reference

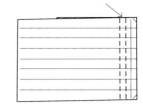

14 Unfold.

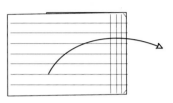

15 Fold between the creases. Unfold.

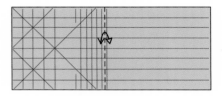

16 Fold edges to the line indicated and crease along the dotted lines shown. Unfold.

Pay attention to the correct reference line

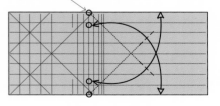

17 Make vertical creases between the points indicated.

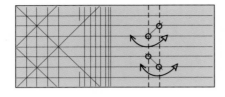

18 Mountain fold the long edges to the center on the back, using existing creases.

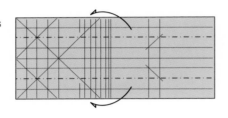

19 Create some new creases, then make the model partially 3-D by collapsing as indicated. The model will not lie flat.

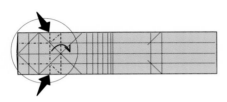

20 Fold as indicated, using existing creases. The model will still not lie flat.

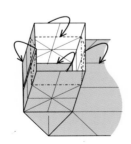

21 Sink the sides and collapse the model flat. See the next step for the result.

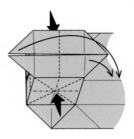

22 Create diagonal creases.

23 Crease vertically through the points indicated.

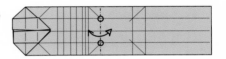

24 Reinforce existing creases (this will crease all the layers). Turn over.

25 Fold edges to the center.

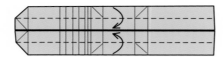

26 Fold the edges to the crease and unfold.

27 Mountain fold at intersection. Unfold.

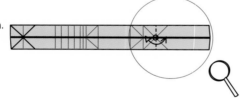

28 Pop the center of the intersection and collapse (it should look something like a waterbomb base).

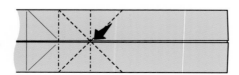

29 Swivel fold the top layer. The model will not lie flat.

Swivel top layer only

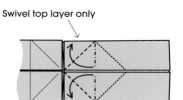

30 Bring the layers together, positioning them so they are perpendicular to the rest of the model. Next step is viewed from the side.

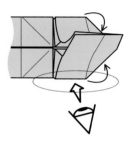

31 Open slightly and mountain fold excess paper so the edge is about level with the rest of the model. This is the bowl and will be adjusted at the end for the proper shape.

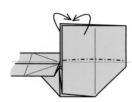

32 Mountain fold the small triangular flaps.

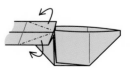

33 View the complete model from above again.

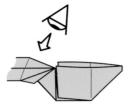

34 Make these creases in preparation for the collapse.

Pay attention to the correct creases to be used.

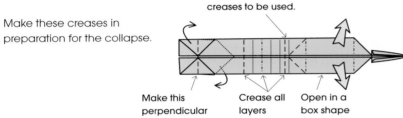

Make this perpendicular

Crease all layers

Open in a box shape

35 Insert the tabs to create the tank.

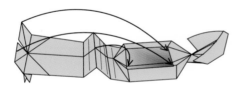

36 Final details next.

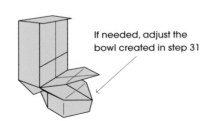

If needed, adjust the bowl created in step 31

37 Fold the lid, seat and the base.

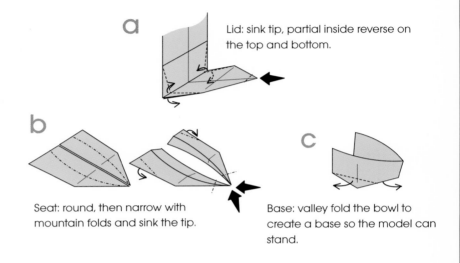

a Lid: sink tip, partial inside reverse on the top and bottom.

b Seat: round, then narrow with mountain folds and sink the tip.

c Base: valley fold the bowl to create a base so the model can stand.

The completed toilet

TANK

You will need to make two units to assemble this model.

Make the tracks first:

1 Fold in half. Unfold.

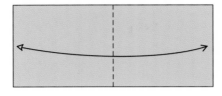

2 Fold the short edge to the long edges diagonally and unfold to crease the angle bisectors. Turn over.

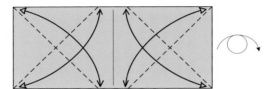

3 Crease at the points indicated.

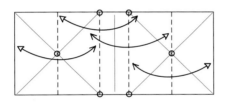

4 Crease between the lines created in the previous step. Turn over.

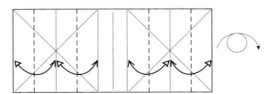

5 Crease between the lines created in the previous step.

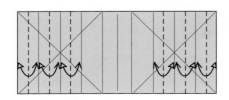

6 Crease between the lines. Turn over.

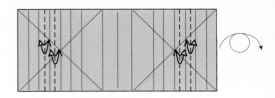

7 Crease between the lines. Turn over.

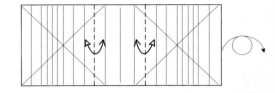

8 Bring edges to the intersections indicated, and crease between the lines only. Turn over.

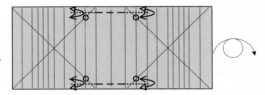

9 Pleat fold. Turn over.

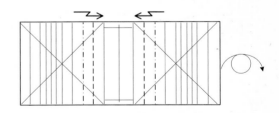

10 Accordion fold.

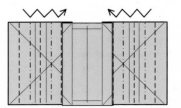

11 Fold all the layers using the existing creases as a reference.

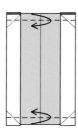

12 The tracks are complete.

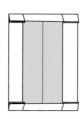

Make the gun turret:

1 Fold the short edge to the long edges and unfold to crease the angle bisectors.

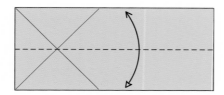

2 Fold in half. Unfold.

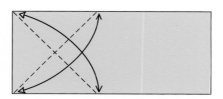

3 Fold edges to the center line and crease up to the diagonals. Turn over.

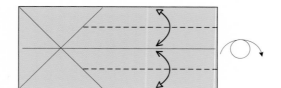

4 Crease between the lines created in the last step, up to the diagonals.

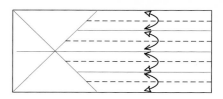

5 Crease vertically through the intersection indicated. Turn over.

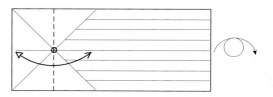

6 Collapse (like a waterbomb base).

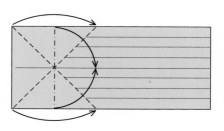

7 Fold edge to the corner and crease. Unfold.

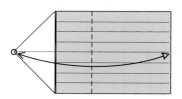

8 Fold edge to the lines shown to create small diagonals. Unfold.

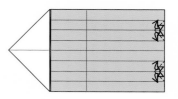

9 Fold vertically through the points indicated. Unfold. Turn over.

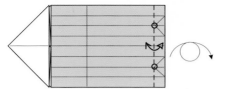

10 Fold the corner, starting at just below the line.

Slightly below the line

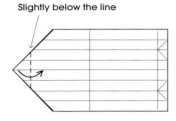

11 Pleat with a mountain fold on the existing crease, bringing the folded edge to the corner.

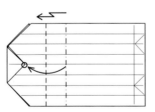

12 Swivel fold.

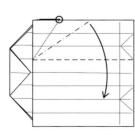

13 Swivel fold.

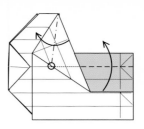

14 Swivel fold.

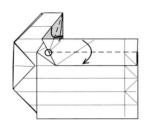

15 Repeat steps 12 to 14 on the other side.

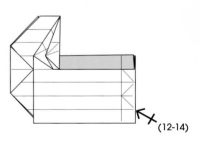

(12-14)

16 Turn over.

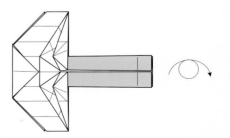

17 Valley fold the top layer only, squashing the middle layers.

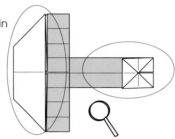

18 Details of the hatch and main gun are next.

19 Fold the hatch:

a Valley fold both flaps.

b Valley fold both flaps.

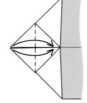

c Rabbit-ear fold one of the flaps and open squash the other.

d Outside reverse fold the flap with the rabbit ear, and mountain fold the open squash.

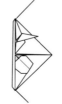

20 Shape the gun:

a Create a small pleat.

(View from bottom)

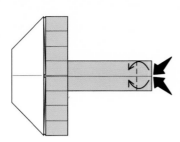

b Form small swivels by the turret and roll the barrel into a tube shape. Turn over.

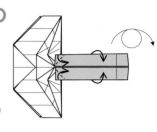

c Viewing from the top, pinch the flaps on each side to create the muzzle brakes. Finish shaping the barrel.

(View from top)

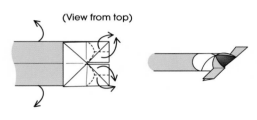

21 Valley fold top layer only, squashing the middle layers.

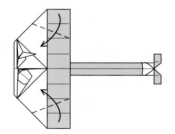

22 Mountain fold, letting the flaps flip out to the sides.

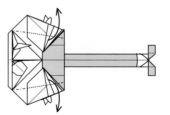

23 Pull the flap out from behind.

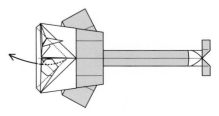

24 Fold and unfold the flaps.

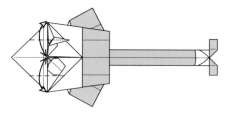

25 Fold under.

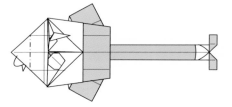

26 Push the flaps up so they stand perpendicular to the hatch and add a rabbit ear on each side. This will help push the back down and give it a tridimensional shape.

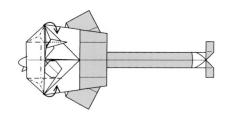

27 Make some dents as indicated and add light mountain creases on the sides to further the tri-dimensional shape.

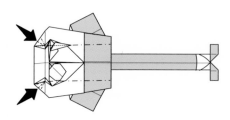

28 The finished turret.

Put the tracks and the turret together:

1 On the tracks unit, push the middle layer inward on the existing crease to make it tridimensional.

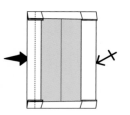

2 Turn over.

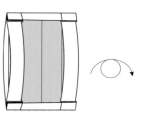

3 Insert the tabs on the turret into the pockets on the tracks unit.

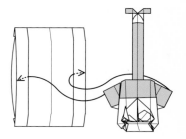

The completed tank

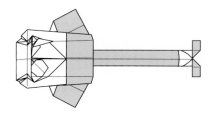

SPIDER

This model requires two units.

1 Fold in half. Unfold.

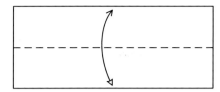

2 Fold in half. Unfold.

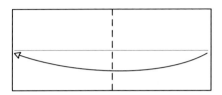

3 On both sides, fold angle bisectors by aligning edge to edge. Unfold.

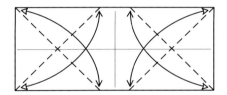

4 Fold and unfold between the points.

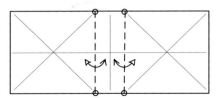

5 Fold and unfold. Turn over.

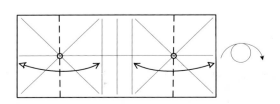

6 Fold angle bisectors. Unfold.

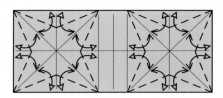

7

a Start collapse.

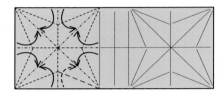

b In progress... add additional creases to move the internal corner.

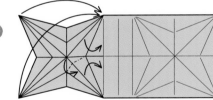

c Fold flat.

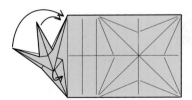

8 Repeat on the other side.

(In progress)

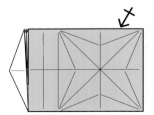

9 Fold both flaps down on both sides. Repeat steps 1 to 9 to make a second unit

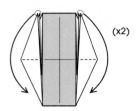

(x2)

10 Turn one of the units over.

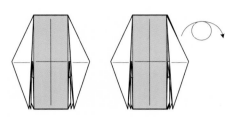

11 Align the units back to back, one on top of the other.

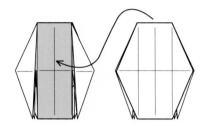

12 Valley fold about ⅓, then valley fold again, rolling over.

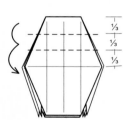

⅓
⅓
⅓

13 Valley fold top flap only.

14 Pleat fold. This will lock the layers on the back.

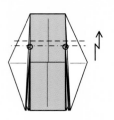

15 Open the model slightly to outside reverse fold.

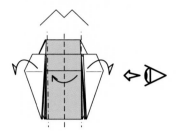

16 Details of the abdomen, legs and fangs next.

Legs   Fangs

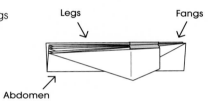

Abdomen

17 Shape jaws and fangs:

a

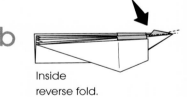

Inside reverse fold.

b

Inside reverse fold.

c

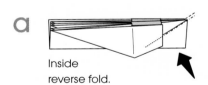

Round to shape.

d

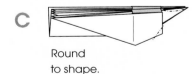

Shaped fangs.

18 Shape legs:

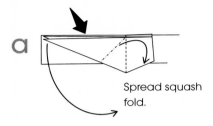

a

Spread squash fold.

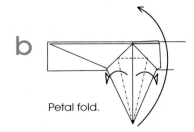

b

Petal fold.

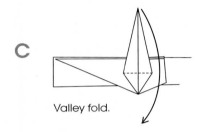

c

Valley fold.

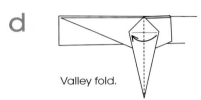

d

Valley fold.

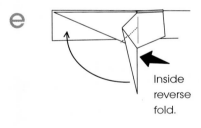

e

Inside reverse fold.

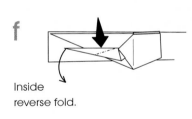

f

Inside reverse fold.

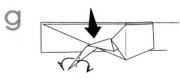

g

Outside reverse fold.

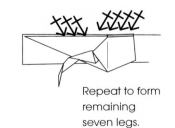

h

Repeat to form remaining seven legs.

19 Shape abdomen:

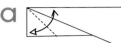

a

Fold and unfold.

b

Fold to the crease.

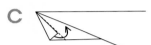

c

Fold on existing creases.

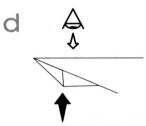

d

Push up from bottom to puff out the abdomen.

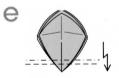

e

Crimp fold to form the spinneret.

The completed spider

FOX

1 Fold in half. Unfold.

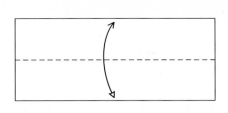

2 Fold in half. Unfold. Turn over.

3 Fold the angle bisectors by aligning crease to crease. Unfold. Turn over.

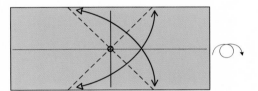

4 Fold between the points and unfold.

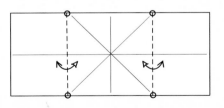

5 Fold angle bisectors as indicated.

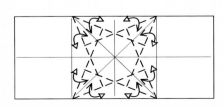

6 Pre-crease: crease the shorter, outer ones well, since they will be used for the sinks in a future step.

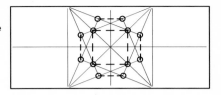

7 Crease well between the points.

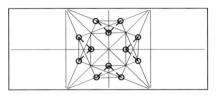

8 Pre-creases are done, ready for the collapse. Turn over. Magnified view for details.

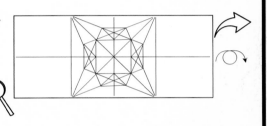

9 Collapse. Visualize a waterbomb base with four open sinks.

Open sink

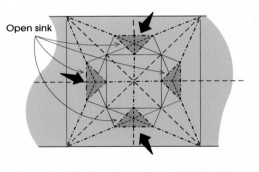

Top view, in progress.

Bottom view, same point in progress.

Note the tip. Move it to either of the sides.

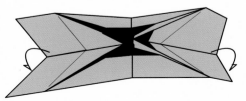

10 Inside reverse.

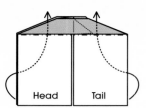

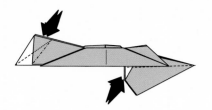

Head | Tail

11 Inside reverse.

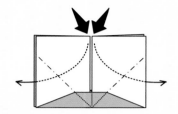

12 Inside reverse.

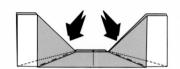

13 Inside reverse.

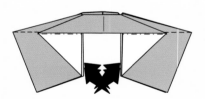

14 Inside reverse. Note the differences between the head and tail sides.

Head | Tail

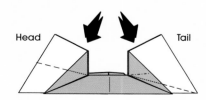

15 Inside reverse.

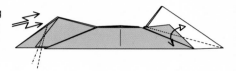

16 Crimp the head, rearranging the layers inside. Fold the tail along the folded edge and unfold.

17 Inside reverse the tail. Note the differences between the head and tail sides.

18 Open the layers on the tail back to step 14.

19 Roll over on existing creases.

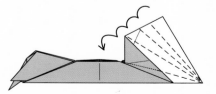

20 Next, details of the legs, tail, and head.

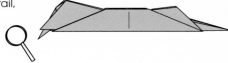

21 Details of the front legs:

a  Valley fold. Repeat on the other side.

b 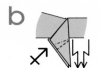 Crimp.

c Inside reverse (only on one leg).

22 Details of the back legs:

a 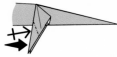 Valley fold.

b  Swivel fold.

c Inside reverse.

d 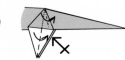  Inside reverse. Repeat a through d on the other side.

23 Details of the head:

a   Valley fold and unfold.

b   Open squash.

c   Petal fold. Repeat steps a through c on the other side.

d   Crimp snout.

e   Crimp neck.

f Tuck corner behind ears to inside.

24 Details of the tail:

a 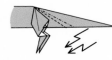 Crimp.

b

The completed fox

PIG

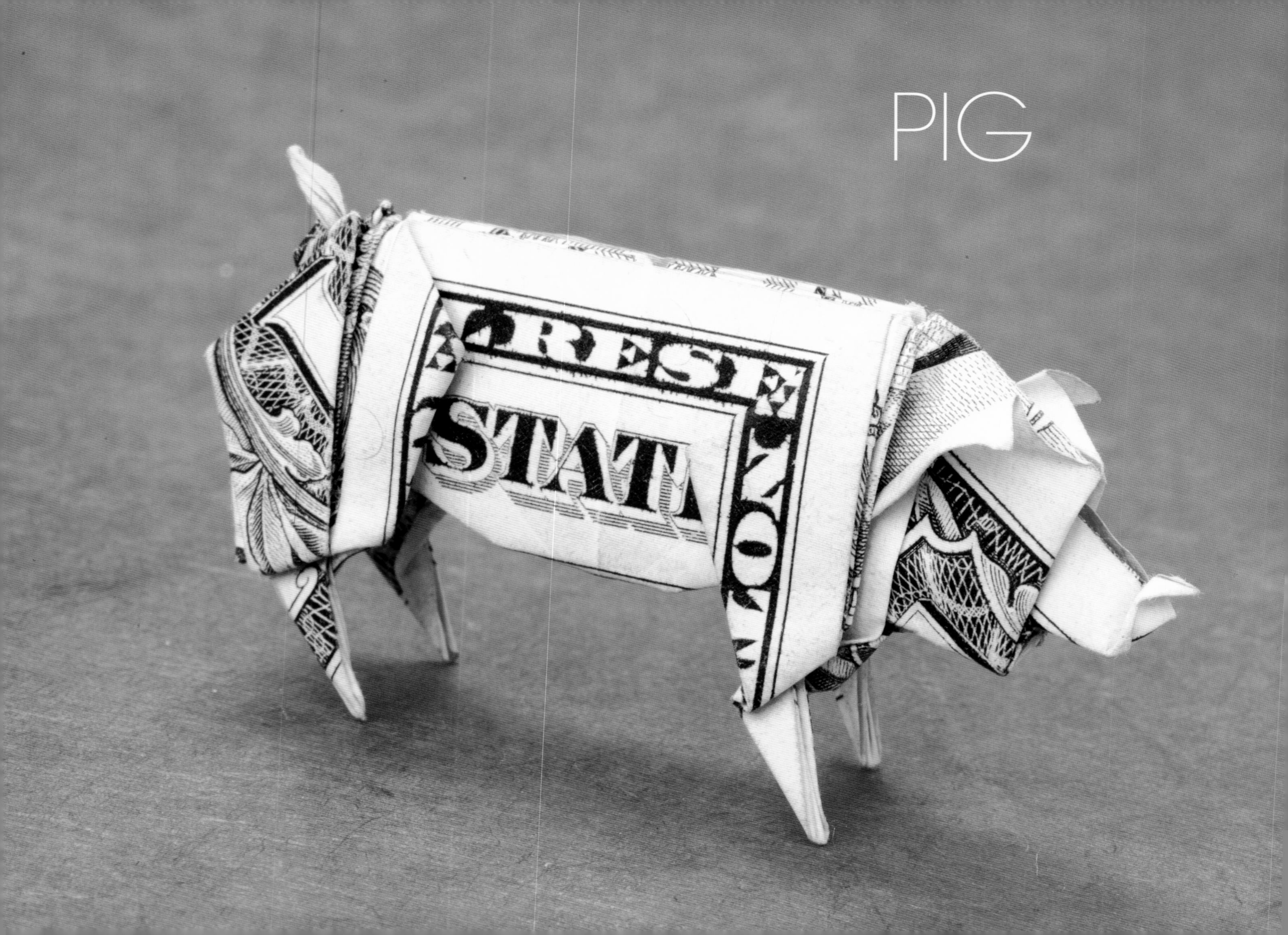

1 Fold in half. Unfold.

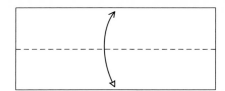

2 Fold the angle bisector by bringing edge to edge; pinch the edge.

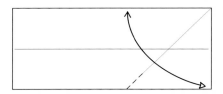

3 Crease starting from the pinch mark.

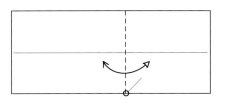

4 Crease the angle bisectors at the intersection.

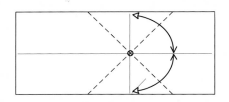

5 Crease between the reference points.

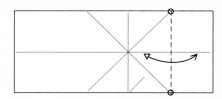

6 Mountain fold the bisectors starting at the points indicated and creasing as far as the diagonal creases. Unfold.

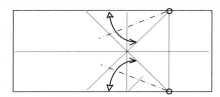

7 Mountain fold at the intersection of the points.

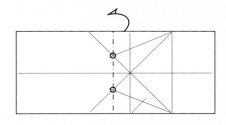

8 Using the crease from the back as a reference, crease the top layer. Note that the short edges will not match.

Align to the crease on the back

Edges will not match

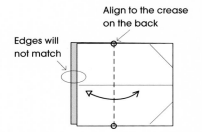

9 Unfold.

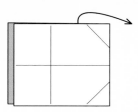

10 Crease the diagonals.

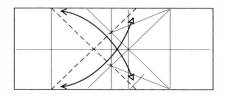

11 Crease the angle bisectors, folding edge to crease, and unfold.

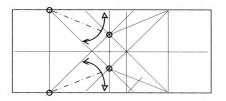

12 Collapse using the creases indicated.

Head side

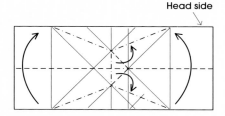

13 Inside reverse fold.

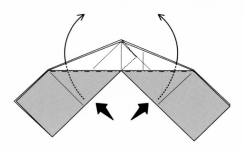

14 Inside reverse fold.

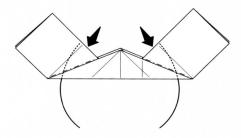

15 Valley fold the top layer of the head side, then repeat on the back. Inside reverse fold on the opposite side.

Head side

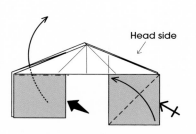

16 Details of the tail next.

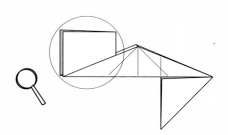

17

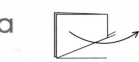

a Open one flap.

b Valley fold.

c Mountain fold excess of paper.

d Fold edge to edge.

e Squash symmetrically.

f Inside reverse fold.

g Close.

18

Crimp.

19

Details of the layers inside.

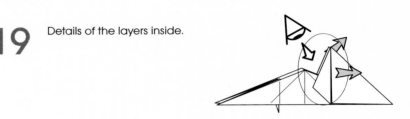

20

Focus on the folded edges. Rearrange the internal layers as indicated.

Focus on the edges

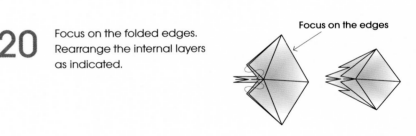

21

Turn the model over.

22 Fold the corner as indicated. Repeat on the back.

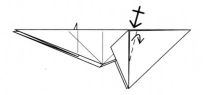

23 Crimp.

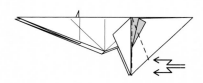

24 Crimp.

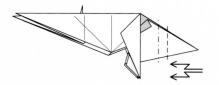

25 Swivel fold on both sides.

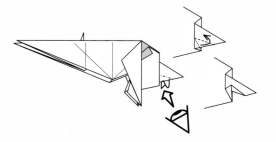

26 Crimp the snout.

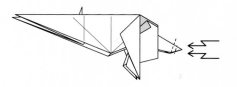

27 Swivel fold. Repeat on the other front leg.

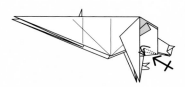

28 Swivel fold the chin (on the inside). Repeat on the back.

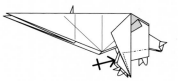

29 Crimp the front leg. Repeat on the other front leg.

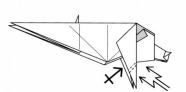

30 Open squash fold. Repeat on other hind leg.

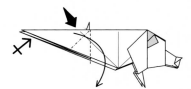

31 Mountain fold inside. Repeat on other hind leg.

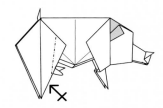

32 Pleat. Repeat on the other hind leg.

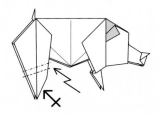

33 Swivel the paper inside.

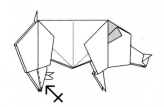

34 Shape by folding the corners of the belly inside and pressing the edges of the legs and back in. Shape the tail.

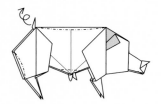

The completed pig

SWORDFISH

1 Fold in half. Unfold.

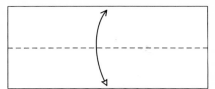

2 Fold the short edge to the long edges diagonally to crease the angle bisectors. Unfold. Turn over.

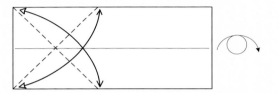

3 Crease at the points indicated.

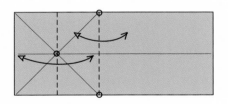

4 Fold the short edge to the long edges diagonally to crease the angle bisectors. Unfold. Turn over.

5 Fold the angle bisectors. Unfold.

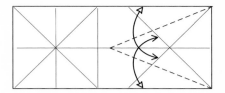

6 Fold edge to the crease indicated and crease between the diagonals. Unfold.

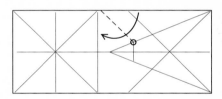

7 Fold at 45° angle. See next step to see how it looks.

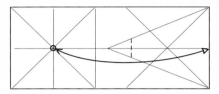

8 Crease between the points indicated only. Unfold.

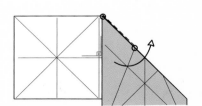

9 Fold at 45° angle. Crease between the points indicated only. Unfold (similar to step 8).

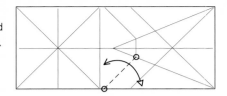

10 Start a new crease from the intersection point by bringing the corner to the crease line indicated.

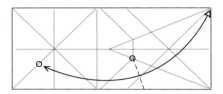

11 Crease between the points indicated only.

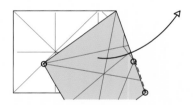

12 Repeat on the other side.

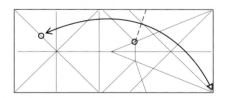

13 Fold between the creases. Unfold.

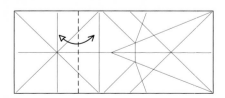

14 Fold between the creases. Unfold.

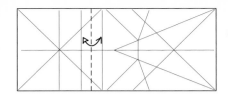

15 Fold between the points indicated. Unfold. Turn over.

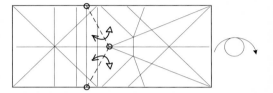

16 Create parallel creases to the ones made in the previous step.

Parallel

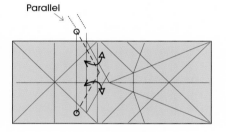

17 Crease the angle bisectors.

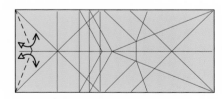

18 Crease the angle bisectors.

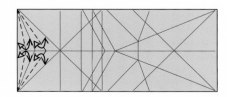

19 Crease the angle bisectors.

20 Fold in half.

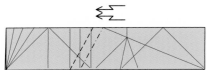

21 Crimp.

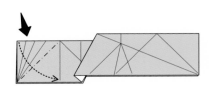

22 Inside reverse fold.

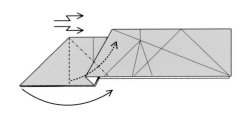

23 Crimp.

24 Inside reverse fold.

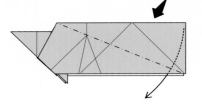

25 Inside reverse fold.

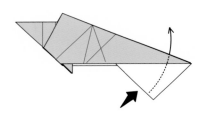

26 Crimp.

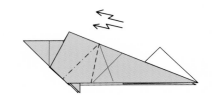

27 Gently open the trapped layer. View from the top.

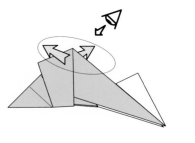

28 Pinch the layers together to flatten. This will result in new creases being formed. See next step for the result.

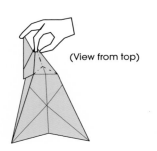

(View from top)

29 Crimp as far as it can go.

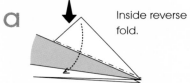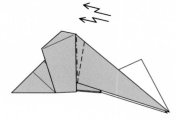

30 Open the top layer to see inside.

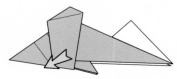

31 Mountain fold a narrow layer inside. Close up the top layer. Repeat on the back.

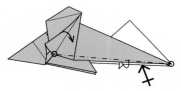

32 Mountain fold, turning under the first layer. Repeat on the back.

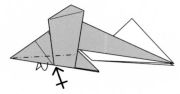

33 Details of the tail fins next.

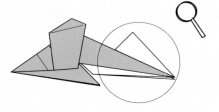

34

a Inside reverse fold.

b Fold the top fin inside and upward.

c Valley fold the bottom fin upward.

d Valley fold the fin tip angled down.

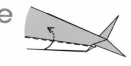

e Tuck the excess paper inside, locking the tail in place.

35 Pull both layers out as far as they go.

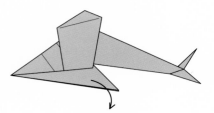

36 Inside reverse the layer from the inside and use the crease as a reference (next step).

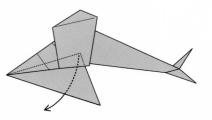

37 Fold the flaps in the front and back up around the middle of the body, then squash them symmetrically.

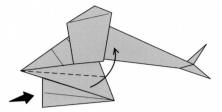

38 Pull the flaps out to the side, like the wings of a plane. View from the bottom.

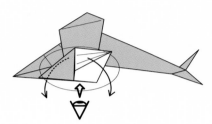

39 Fold edges to the center, then bring the point forward as indicated. Return the flaps to the original position.

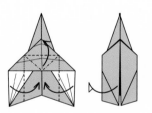

40 Mountain fold along the edge and open the flap slightly to the side. It will not lie flat. Repeat on the back.

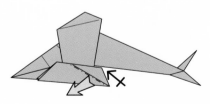

41 Tuck inside, pull some paper from inside, and create a new flap with a valley fold. Repeat on the back.

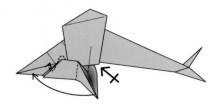

42 Valley fold the flap toward the back. Repeat on the other side to make matching pectoral fins.

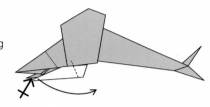

43 Create a sequence of mountain and valley creases to form the sail, shape the bill and head, and then pull the mouth open.

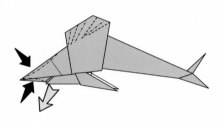

The completed swordfish

SEA TURTLE

1 Fold in half. Unfold.

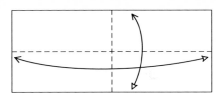

2 Fold edges to crease and unfold.

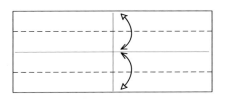

3 Fold edges to the creases indicated and unfold.

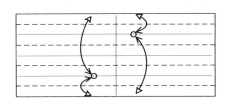

4 Fold the short edges to the long edges and unfold to crease the angle bisectors.

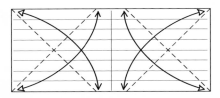

5 Crease through the reference points indicated and unfold. Turn over.

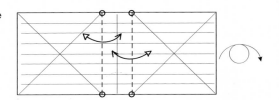

6 Fold edges to the creases. Unfold. Turn over.

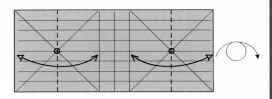

7 Fold edges to the middle creases and unfold. Turn over.

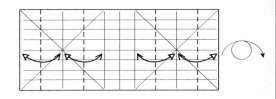

8 Fold between the folded edges. Unfold. Turn over.

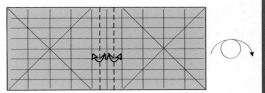

9 Pleat by bringing the creases formed in the previous step to the center.

New creases

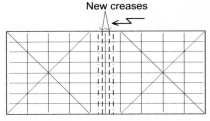

10 Collapse the waterbomb bases on both sides.

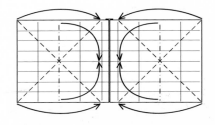

11 Open sink the corners.

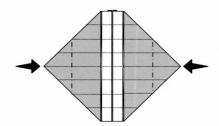

12 Turn over.

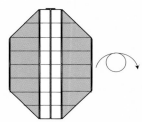

13 Pleat fold the top layer only, forming new creases as indicated.

New creases

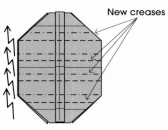

14 Turn over.

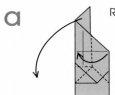

15 Fold edges to the center.

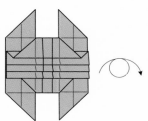

16 Details of the front and hind flippers, head, and tail next. Helpful: use tweezers to make tiny, hard-to-grasp folds.

Front flippers
Head
Tail
Hind flippers

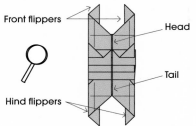

17 Details of the left front flipper:

a Rabbit-ear fold.

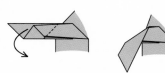

b

Valley fold. Repeat steps a and b on the right front flipper.

18 Details of the left hind flipper:

a Valley fold edge to edge (tuck under the layer).

b Valley fold.

c Valley fold.

d

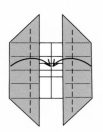

Crimp. Repeat steps a to d on the right hind flipper.

19 Details of the head (under the front flippers):

a

Push the pleat and open slightly.

b

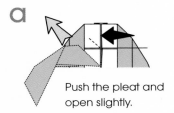

Continue pushing to form new creases as indicated for a swivel.

c

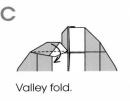

Valley fold.

d

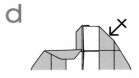

Repeat steps a to c on the other side.

20 Valley fold (under the hind flippers). See details of the tail next.

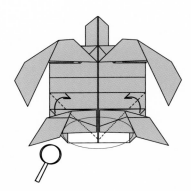

21 Details of the tail (under the hind flippers):

a

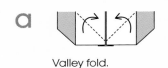

Valley fold.

b

Push to form new creases as indicated to fold flat.

22 Bring layer to the top (hind flippers will move inside).

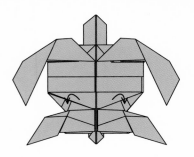

23 Turn over.

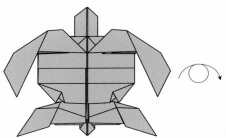

24 Shape the model: make the head tridimensional by opening up the layers and rounding the eyes. Adjust the pleats on the back to simulate the pattern on the shell.

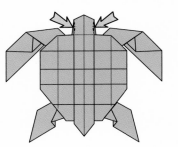

The completed sea turtle

OX

If you fold this model with a one-dollar bill, be sure to start with the face (white) side up so that the printed pattern on the bill will make the eyes. This does not apply to bills of other denominations.

1 Fold in half. Unfold.

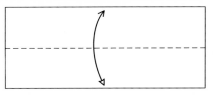

2 Fold the angle bisectors by bringing the short edge to the long edges. Unfold. Turn over.

3 Crease between the reference points indicated.

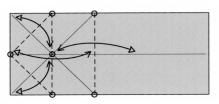

4 Fold and unfold.

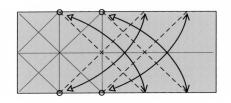

5 Fold and unfold. Turn over.

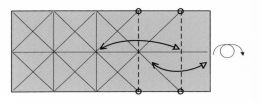

6 Crease the angle bisectors. Turn over.

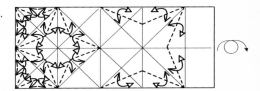

7 Crease between the points and crease the angle bisectors.

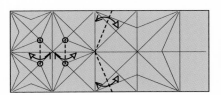

8 Collapse using the creases indicated.

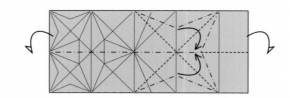

9 Collapse using the creases indicated.

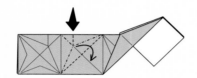

10 Collapse using the creases indicated.

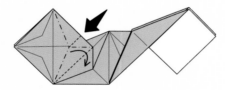

11 Collapse using the creases indicated.

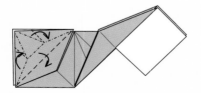

12 Rabbit-ear fold.

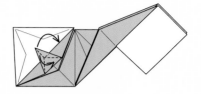

13 Repeat steps 11 and 12 on the other side.

(11-12)

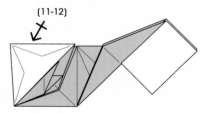

14 Crimp.

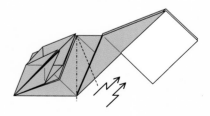

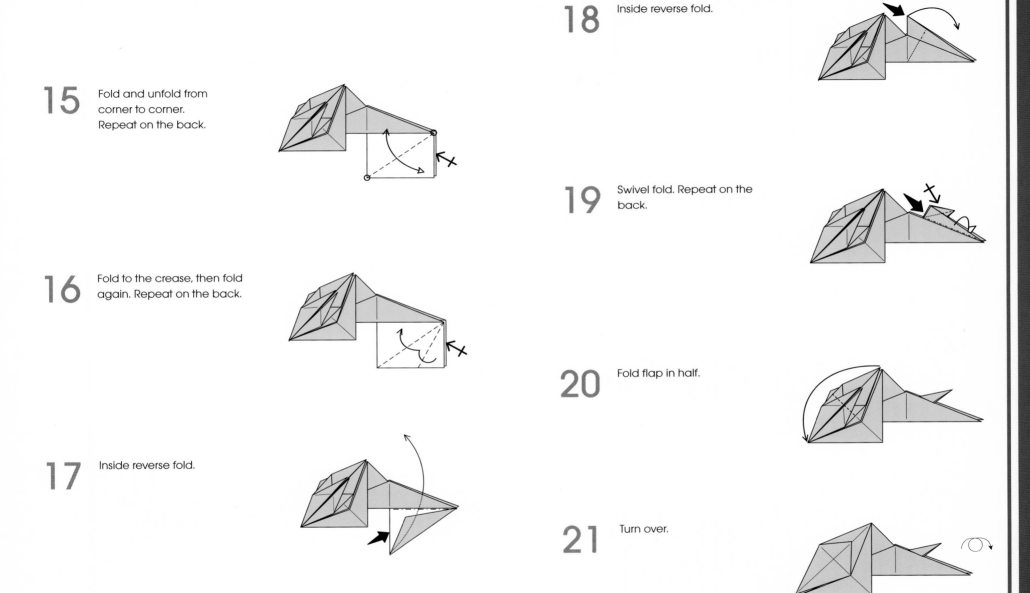

15 Fold and unfold from corner to corner. Repeat on the back.

16 Fold to the crease, then fold again. Repeat on the back.

17 Inside reverse fold.

18 Inside reverse fold.

19 Swivel fold. Repeat on the back.

20 Fold flap in half.

21 Turn over.

22 Valley fold.

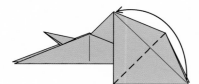

23 Valley fold.

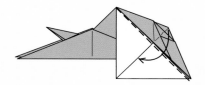

24 Turn over.

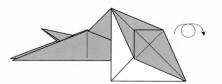

25 Valley fold. Turn over.

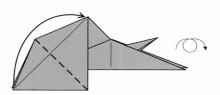

26 Collapse the head in this order: Valley fold (1), mountain fold (2), and then press the forehead area (3) up against the neck. The printed pattern should provide a reference for the forehead and a suggestion of the eyes.

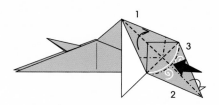

27 Fold and unfold the back under the flaps.

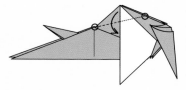

28 Open sink the back.

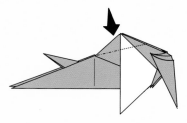

29 Details of the head and hind legs are next.

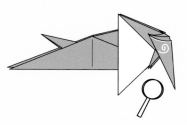

30 Start shaping head details:

a

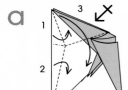 

Shape the horns in this order: (1) Fold the edge to the edge. (2) Extend the crease to the corner. (3) Fold down the flap to make it flat. Repeat steps a (1), (2), and (3) on the other side.

b

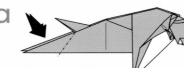

Narrow the horn by shifting some paper. Repeat on the back.

c

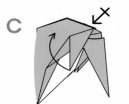

Curl both horns.

d

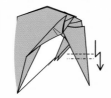

Pleat muzzle.

e

Fold under.

f

Inside reverse the ears.

g

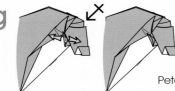

Petal fold to open the ears.

31 Shape the hind legs:

a

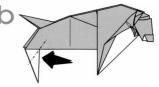

Inside reverse. Repeat on the back.

b

Inside reverse. Repeat on the back.

c

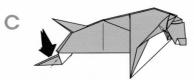

Inside reverse. Repeat on the back.

32 Crimp the foreleg to narrow it. Repeat on the other side. Shape the nose on both sides.

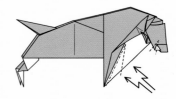

The completed ox

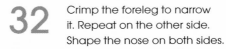

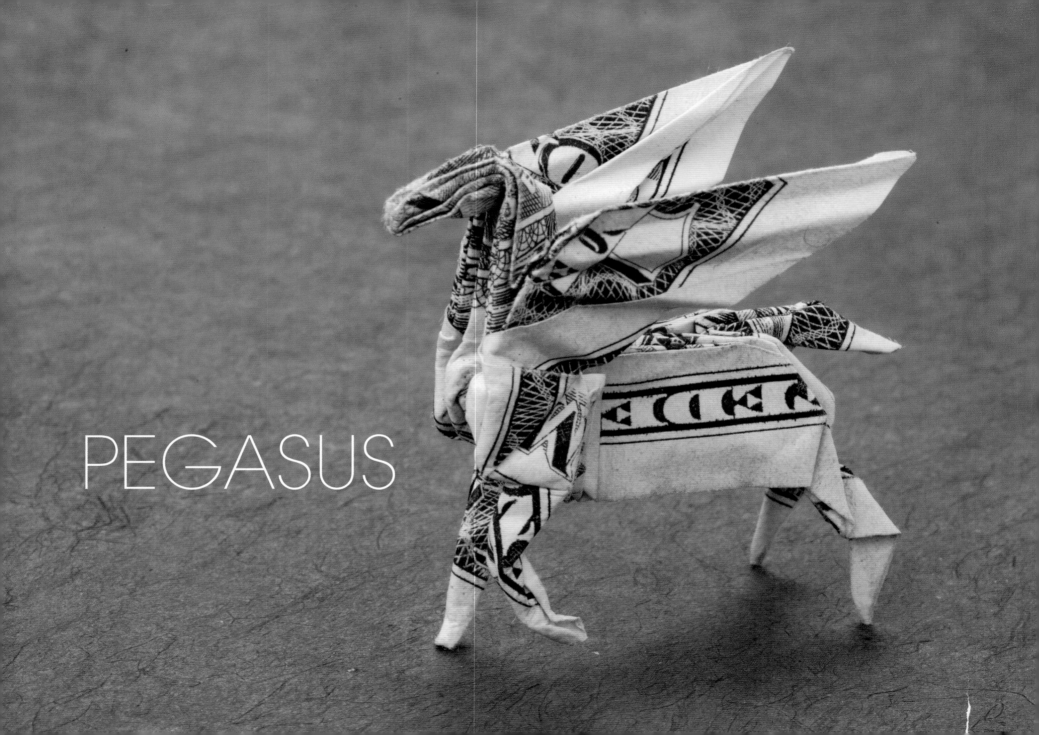

PEGASUS

1 Fold in half lengthwise. Unfold.

2 Fold edge to edge.

3 Execute in this order: (1) Fold edge to edge and unfold. (2) Unfold the previous flap.

4 Repeat the previous steps on the other side. Turn over.

5 Valley fold vertically through the intersection of the creases. Unfold.

6 Fold edges to the creases, creating angle bisectors. Unfold.

7 Valley fold between the reference points.

8 Mountain fold between the reference points.

9 Valley fold angle bisectors as indicated.

10 Pre-crease. Crease the shorter, outer folds well since these will be used for the sinks.

11 Pre-crease well.

12 Pre-creases done and ready for the collapse. Turn over. Magnified view for the details.

13 Collapse. Visualize a waterbomb base with three open sinks.

Open sink

Leave this unsunk

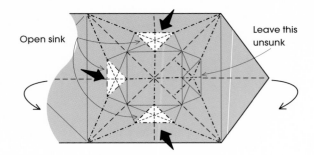

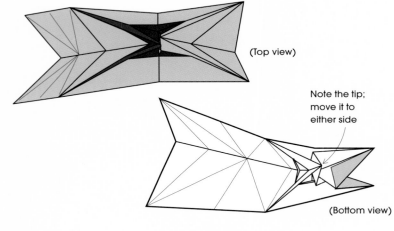

(Top view)

Note the tip; move it to either side

(Bottom view)

14 Detailed view.

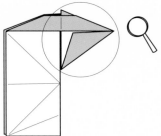

15 Open the flap.

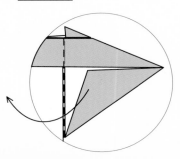

16 Closed sink, using existing creases.

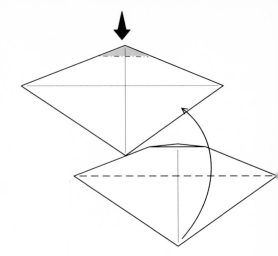

17 Fold the flap up.

18 Crease along the edge on the back.

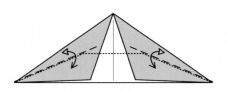

19 Execute in this order: (1) Fold down flap. (2) Close flap. The result will look similar to the position in step 14.

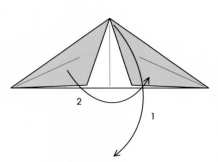

20 Inside reverse fold. Fold edge to the corner indicated.

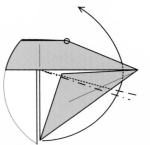

21 Inside reverse fold. Fold corner to the crease.

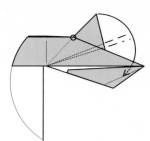

22 Move up the crimp on existing creases, keeping the last inside reverse in place.

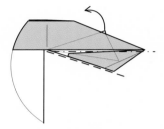

23 Swivel, first along the long edge, and then flatten the flap. Repeat on the back.

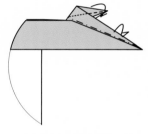

24 Swivel. Repeat on the back.

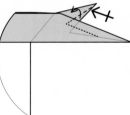

25 Tail complete.

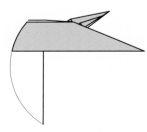

26 Inside reverse fold on existing creases.

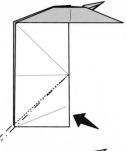

27 Inside reverse fold inside the flap using existing creases.

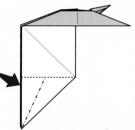

28 Inside reverse fold inside the flap, now creating new creases. Align the cut edge with the folded edge.

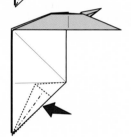

29 Inside reverse fold, refolding into a waterbomb-base shape. Keep the inside reverse folds created in the previous step in place.

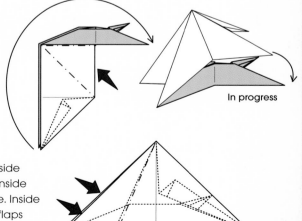

In progress

30 The body and the inside reverse folds are all inside the waterbomb base. Inside reverse fold the two flaps indicated.

31 Fold flap on existing crease. Note that it will not lie flat.

32 Fold in at an angle, pivoting from the folded edge and adjusting the inside reverse folds so that the model will lie flat.

(31-32)

33 Repeat steps 31 and 32 on the back.

34 Asymmetrical inside reverse fold. Repeat behind.

35 Inside reverse fold under the flap. Repeat behind.

36 Fold the edge along the edge. Note that it will not come to a point at the wingtip. Repeat behind.

37 Mountain fold the top layer under. Repeat behind.

38 Asymmetrical inside reverse fold. Repeat behind.

39 Shaping details are shown in the next steps.

40 Inside reverse fold the head. Fold the tip inside to shape the muzzle.

41 Fold the top layer inside to narrow the neck. Repeat behind. Fold the middle thick layer inside. Repeat behind.

42 The head and neck details are complete. Next, shaping details of the forelegs.

43 Details of the left foreleg (raised):

a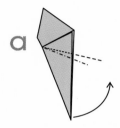

Inside reverse.

b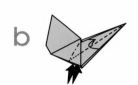

Inside reverse on the front and back.

c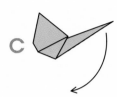

Fold the flap down.

d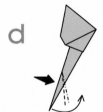

Inside reverse.

e

Inside reverse.

44 For the right foreleg, follow steps 43 a through c, adjusting the angle so the leg is straight.

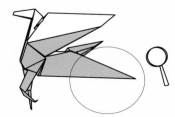

45 Details of the hind legs (steps are shown without the tail for clarity):

a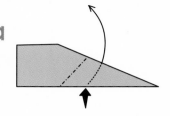

Inside reverse.

b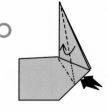

Inside reverse front and back.

c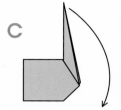

Fold flap down.

d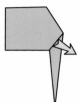

Release some trapped paper.

e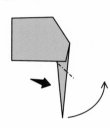

Inside reverse.

f

Inside reverse.

46 Final shaping details: pleat the wings and curl the tail to give it some flow.

The completed Pegasus

PRAYING MANTIS

1 Fold in half. Unfold.

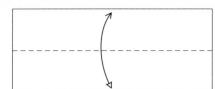

2 Fold the angle bisectors by bringing edge to edges and edges to crease. Unfold. Turn over.

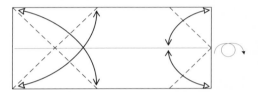

3 Crease between the reference points indicated. Turn over.

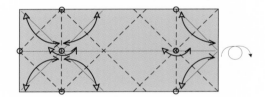

4 Fold through the reference points and unfold.

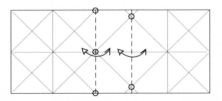

5 Crease the angle bisectors.

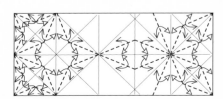

6 Fold in half.

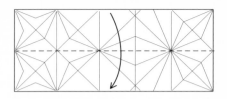

7 Using the existing creases, fold as indicated.

(On the back)

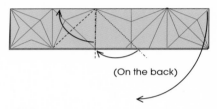

8 Push where indicated and collapse flat. Allow the paper to wrap around by the edge.

Be careful here

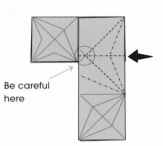

9 Collapse the angle bisectors. Repeat on the back.

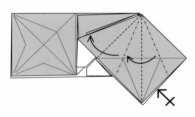

10 Fold one flap.

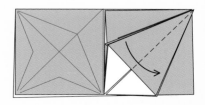

11 Petal fold.

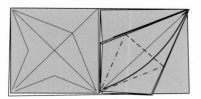

12 Fold flap back to its original position.

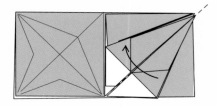

13 Repeat steps 10 to 12 on the other side.

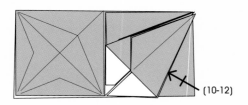

(10-12)

14 Turn over.

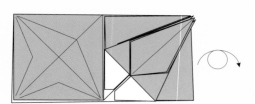

15 Push where indicated and collapse flat half of a bird base. A new crease will form.

New crease

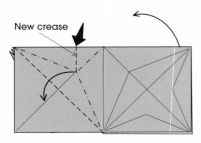

16 Push where indicated and collapse flat the other half of a bird base. A new crease will form.

New crease

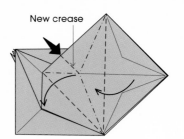

17 At this point, the unit should be completely symmetrical. Rotate 45°.

45°

18 Valley fold one flap.

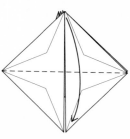

19 Inside reverse fold.

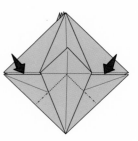

20 Inside reverse fold on existing creases.

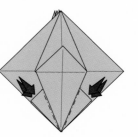

21 Valley fold the group of small flaps that was created in the previous step.

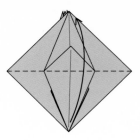

22 Turn over.

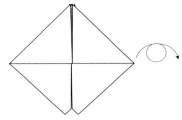

23 Fold edge to the center. Crease it well. Unfold.

Crease is about 2 mm off from corner

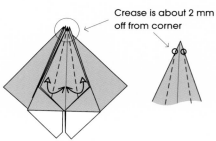

24 Open sink on the creases made in the previous step.

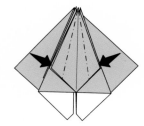

25 Open sink the layer below by repeating steps 23 to 24 on both sides.

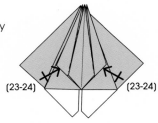

(23-24)   (23-24)

26 Valley fold under the layers.

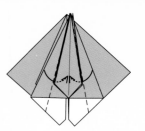

27 Fold the group of large and small flaps behind.

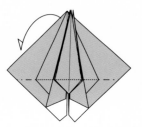

28 Tuck the tabs inside the pocket.

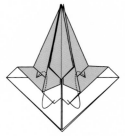

29 Valley fold top layer only. The paper on the top will not lie flat.

Will not lie flat

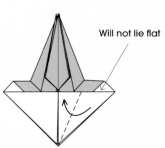

30 Push the paper to allow it to lie flat. This will form new creases. See next step for result.

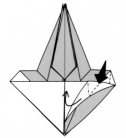

31 Repeat steps 29 and 30 on the other side.

(29-30)

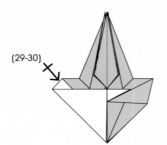

32 Turn over.

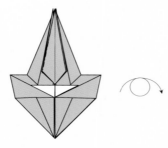

33 Valley fold flaps slightly off from the corner.

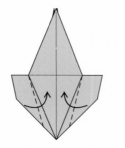

34 Turn over.

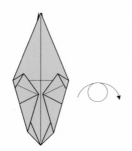

35 Fold the layers under. Use clamps on the thick layers to hold paper flat.

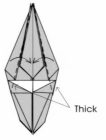

Thick

36 Details of the walking legs, forelegs and head next. Helpful: use tweezers to make tiny, hard-to-grasp folds.

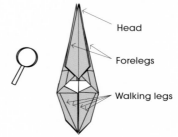

Head

Forelegs

Walking legs

37 Details of left walking leg:

a

Open squash.

b

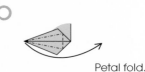

Petal fold.

c

Valley fold.

d

Valley fold. Repeat steps a through d on the other three legs.

38

Details of the left foreleg:

a

Crimp.

b

Inside reverse.

c

Valley fold both layers inward. Repeat steps a through c on the other foreleg.

39

Details of the head:

a

Crimp.

b

Open the layers to form eyes.

40

Create the jointed walking legs and shape. Turn over.

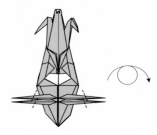

41

Crimp the base of the neck.

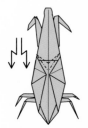

The completed praying mantis

STAG BEETLE

1 Fold in half. Unfold.

2 Fold the angle bisectors by bringing the short edge to the long edges. Unfold. Turn over.

3 Crease between the reference points indicated.

4 Crease the angle bisectors and unfold. Turn over.

5 Crease the angle bisectors and unfold. Turn over.

6 Repeat steps 2 to 5 on the opposite side. (Note: the creases will be inverted.)

(On opposite side)   (2-5)

7 Valley fold between the creases. Unfold. Turn over.

8 Valley fold between the creases. Unfold.

9 Valley fold and unfold.

10 Fold in half.

11 Push where indicated and collapse flat into one half of a bird base. A new crease will be formed.

New crease

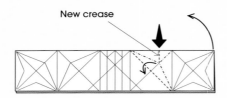

12 Push where indicated and collapse flat into the other half of a bird base. A new crease will be formed.

New crease

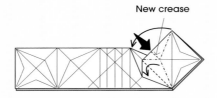

13 Valley fold the top layer only.

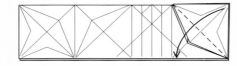

14 On the back layer, fold the point indicated to the corner. The model will not lie flat. View from the top.

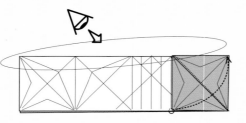

15 Pleat. See next step for details on the top.

Point from previous step

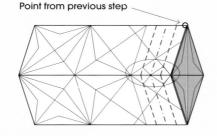

16

a Basic pleat, pushing the flaps to each side.

OR

b A more elegant pleat, requiring new creases (technique used by Won Park).

Pleat

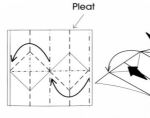

Pleat

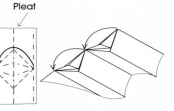

17 Pop the center and prepare for the next collapse by reinforcing the creases indicated.

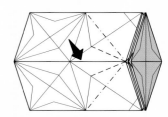

18 Collapse into half of an upside-down bird base. Swing the flap to the right side. At this point the model should lie flat. View from the side next.

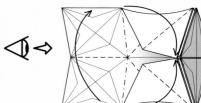

19 Push where indicated and collapse into the other half of an upside-down bird base. A new crease will form.

New crease

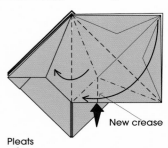

20 Fold top layer only.

Pleats   Pleats

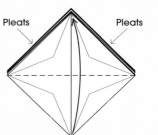

21 Inside reverse.

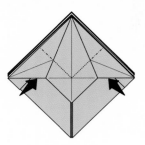

22 Inside reverse on existing creases.

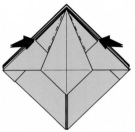

23 Open sink.

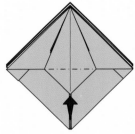

24 Turn over.

25 Repeat steps 21 to 24 on the bottom side.

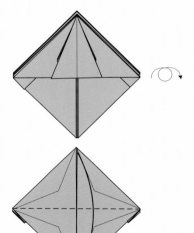

(21-24)

26 Valley fold one flap.

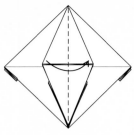

27 Valley fold edge to the center.

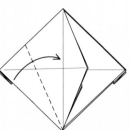

28 Open squash.

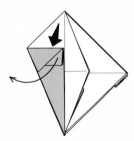

29 Swivel fold.

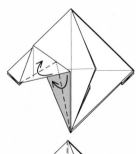

30 Fold flap back to its original position.

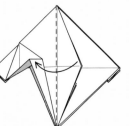

31 Repeat steps 26 to 30 on the other side.

(26-30)

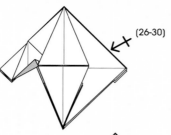

32 Turn over.

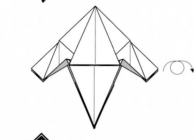

33 Fold the flap down.

34 Valley fold edges to the center and open squash the pleats. See next step for the result.

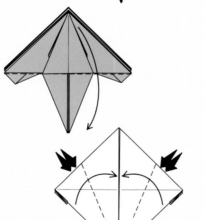

35 Mountain fold the small flaps and tuck them under.

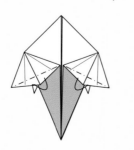

36 Valley fold.

37 Valley fold the top flap only.

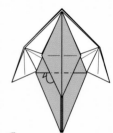

38 Mountain fold and tuck the flap inside.

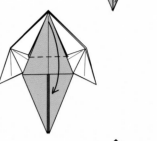

39 Details of the legs are next.

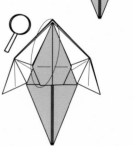

40 Start with the left leg:

a   b   c   d

Open squash.   Petal fold.   Valley fold.   Valley fold.

41 Repeat on the other legs.

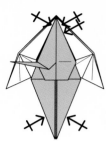

42 Turn over.

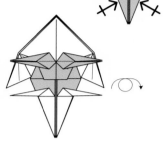

43 Valley fold the top flap only.

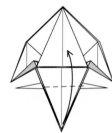

44 Mountain fold and tuck the flap inside.

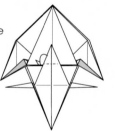

45 Valley fold and tuck the corners inside.

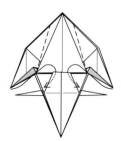

46 Details of the pincers are next.

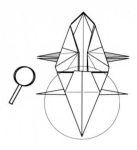

47 Fold the pincers:

a

Inside reverse.

b

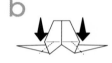

Inside reverse.

c

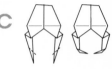

Outside reverse.

48 Inside reverse to shape jointed legs. Press to open the eyes.

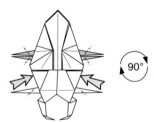

90°

The completed stag beetle

CAR

You will need two pieces of paper for this model, one for the body and one for the chassis.

Make the car body:

1 Fold in half. Unfold.

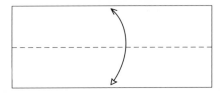

2 Fold in quarters. Unfold.

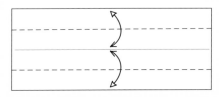

3 Fold the eighths. Unfold.

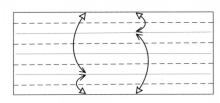

4 Crease between the creases.

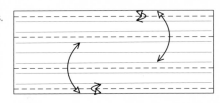

5 Fold short edge along the longs edges to make the angle bisectors.

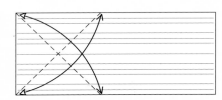

6 Valley fold between the reference points.

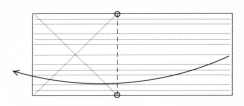

7 Valley fold using the short edge on the back as a guide. Unfold.

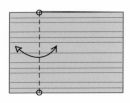

8 Unfold back to step 6.

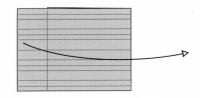

9 Crease between the vertical lines.

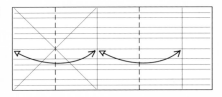

10 Crease between the lines.

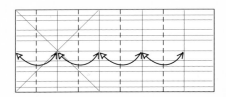

11 Crease between the lines.

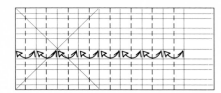

12 Valley fold on existing crease.

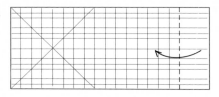

13 Valley fold using the crease on the back as a guide. Unfold.

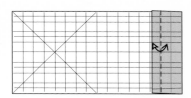

14 Unfold back to step 13.

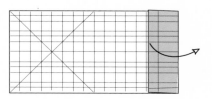

15 Crease between the lines.

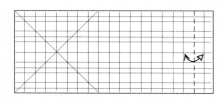

16 Crease between the lines. Turn over.

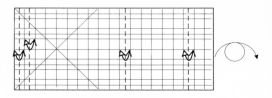

17 Crease between the lines.

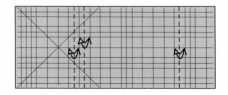

18 Pinch between the creases by the edges only.

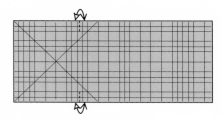

19 Crease between the reference points indicated.

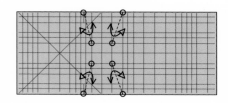

20 Crease between the reference points indicated. Turn over.

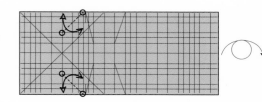

21 Crease between the reference points indicated.

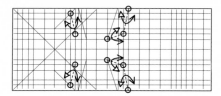

22 Pinch between the creases close to the edges.

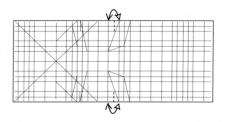

23 Crease between the reference points indicated.

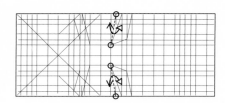

24 Fold the horizontal valley creases indicated, then swing the flap inward. This will create mountain creases.

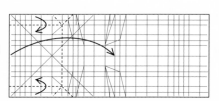

25 Inside reverse and swing the flap outward.

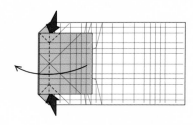

26 Pleat fold.

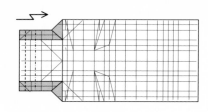

27 Inside reverse.

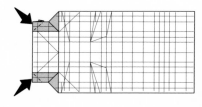

28 Valley fold.

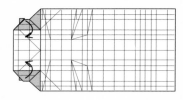

29 Release paper trapped.

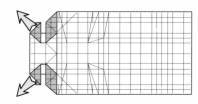

30 The next steps are similar to steps 24 to 28. Fold the horizontal valley creases indicated, then swing the flap inward. This will create mountain creases.

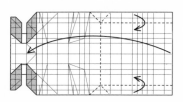

31 Inside reverse and swing the flap outward.

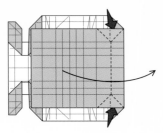

32 Pleat fold.

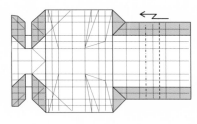

33 Inside reverse.

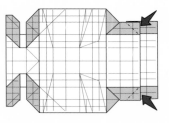

34 Valley fold.

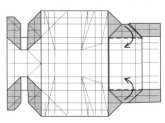

35 Turn over.

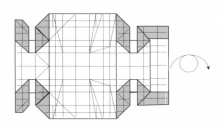

36 Make the body tridimensional: (1) Crimp along the sides. (2) Valley fold to form windshields. (3) Fold mountain creases along doors, trunk and hood to shape.

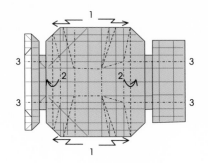

37 Mountain fold edges inside to maintain shape.

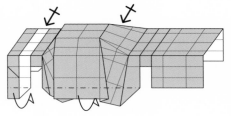

38 Crimp.

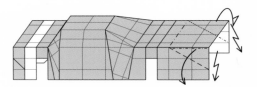

39 Crimp.

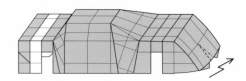

40 Mountain fold along a curve to shape the fenders.

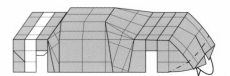

41 Make fenders with curved mountain folds. Push lightly to shape the hood.

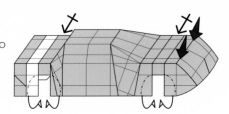

The car body is complete.

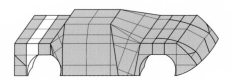

Make the chassis:

1 Fold in half. Unfold.

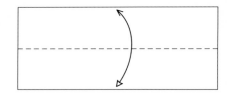

2 Fold in quarters. Unfold.

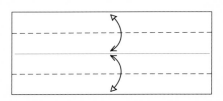

3 Fold the eighths. Unfold.

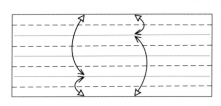

4 Crease between the lines (the sixteenths). Unfold.

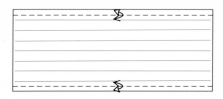

5 Fold short edge along the long edges to make the angle bisectors.

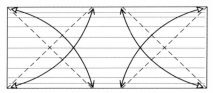

6 Valley fold between the points indicated. Only the left part will be shown for next steps, for clarity. But all steps should be repeated on the right side, too.

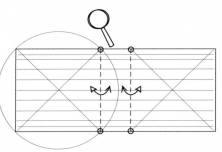

7 Crease between the lines.

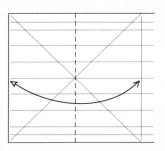

8 Crease between the lines.

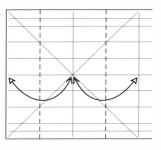

9 Crease between the lines. Turn over.

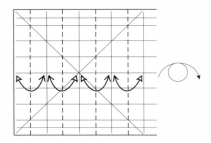

10 Crease between the lines. Turn over.

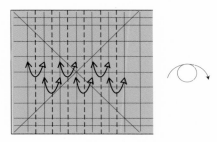

11 Crease between the lines. Turn over.

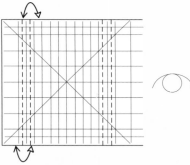

12 Crease between the lines. Turn over.

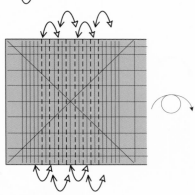

13 Crease the short diagonals. Turn over.

Third crease from right/left

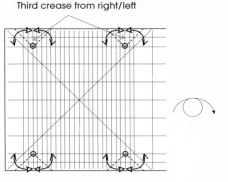

14 Fold a narrow hem, then pleat.

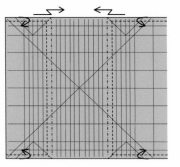

15 Valley fold, open sink on the third crease from the left/right, and fold inward.

Open sink on third crease from left/right

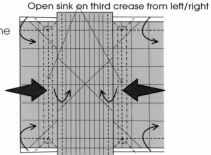

16 Sequence of pleats. Next steps show both sides.

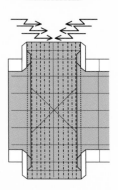

17 Pleat.

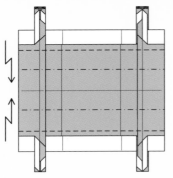

18 Valley fold the flaps along the folded edges. Helpful: Use clamps overnight to maintain the shape.

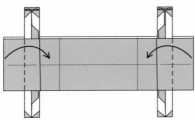

19 Details of the wheels next.

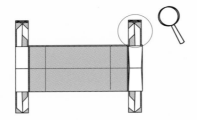

20 Make a wheel:

a

Open the layers slightly.

b

Squash from inside to round.

c

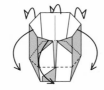

Fold edge to the outside. Helpful: Use tweezers to execute this fold.

21 Repeat on remaining wheels.

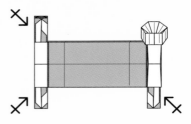

The chassis is complete.

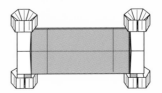

Assemble the car:

Place the car body on top of the finished chassis.

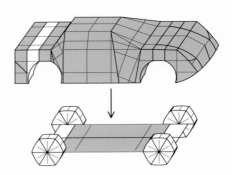

The completed car

FIGHTER JET

1 Fold in half. Unfold.

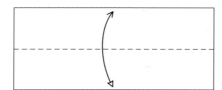

2 Fold edges to the crease and unfold.

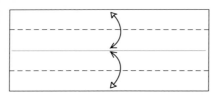

3 Fold edges to the new creases and unfold.

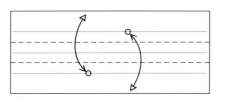

4 Fold short edge to the long edges and unfold to crease the angle bisectors.

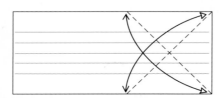

5 Crease at the points indicated.

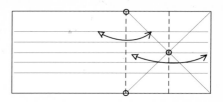

6 Fold the edge to the crease and unfold.

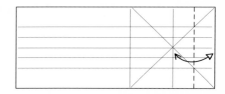

7 Fold the edge to the crease and unfold.

8 Crease between the folded edges. (Note: bring the folded edge to folded edge on the back to form this crease line.)

9 Fold edge to the crease formed in the last step (indicated). Turn over.

10 Fold edge to the crease formed in the last step (indicated).

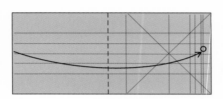

11 Crease, using the crease on the layer below as a guide.

Use crease from layer below as reference

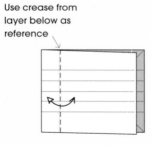

12 Unfold back to step 10.

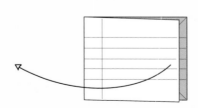

13 Fold edge to the crease indicated, creasing between the lines only. Unfold.

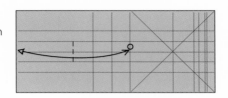

14 Fold edge to the crease indicated, creasing between the lines only. Unfold.

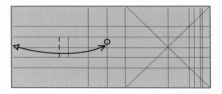

15 Fold between the last two creases. Turn over.

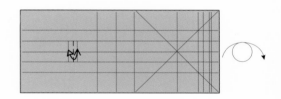

16 Pleat fold using existing creases.

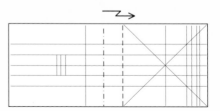

17 Inside reverse: use existing long crease, then form a new one from corner to corner shown. The last crease will be formed when the model is flattened (see next step for result).

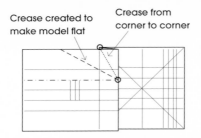

Crease created to make model flat

Crease from corner to corner

18 Turn over.

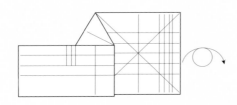

19 Crease the angle bisectors.

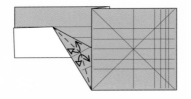

20 While folding the angle bisectors, form a new crease from folded edge to the crease in the middle as indicated. The model will not lie flat.

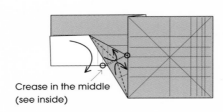

Crease in the middle (see inside)

21 Repeat steps 17 to 20 on the other side.

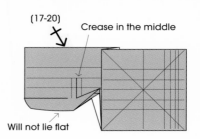

(17-20)

Crease in the middle

Will not lie flat

22 Collapse the model to make it lie flat. New creases will be formed on the sides and the tail end will fold along the crease in the middle.

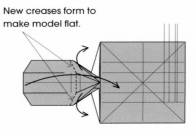

New creases form to make model flat.

23 Outside reverse fold.

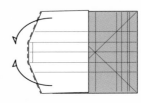

24 Turn over.

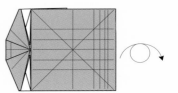

25 Valley fold using the reference points underneath (the intersection of the folded edges).

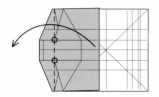

26 Turn over.

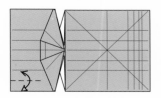

27 Fold edge to crease part way. Unfold.

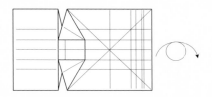

28 Fold edge to new crease. Unfold.

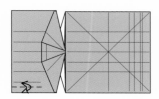

29 Fold edge to crease. Unfold.

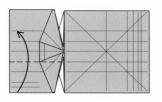

30 Open squash and flatten all layers.

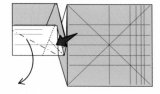

31 Mountain fold on the existing crease.

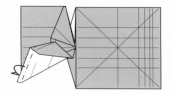

32 Repeat steps 27 to 31 on the other side.

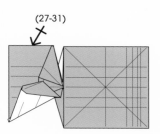

33 Fold the flaps so they stand up.

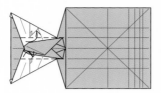

34 Details of the tail stabilizers next. Start collapse by folding the layers toward the inside.

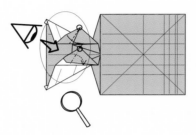

35 Make all folds that are close to the fuselage so that it becomes a single layer, then pinch to flatten. Then form additional parallel creases shown.

Pinch, and bring edge to the perpendicular crease.

Parallel creases

Align edges

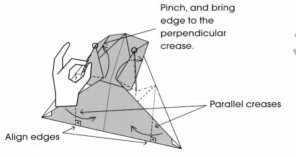

36 Details of the tail flap.

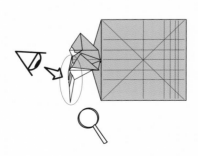

37 Fold diagonally to the back.

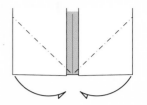

38 Fold flap to the bottom. View from underneath.

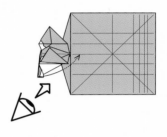

39 Tuck inside the pocket.

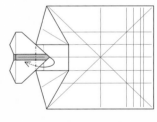

40 Fold edge to crease and tuck small pleats inside.

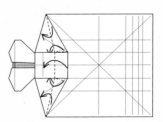

41 Fold edges to the creases indicated. Unfold.

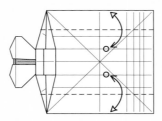

42 Fold edges to the new creases formed in the last step.

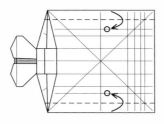

43 Fold diagonally using the references indicated. See next picture for result.

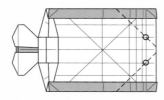

44 Mountain fold between the creases and unfold. This is a partial pre-crease that will be used for a collapse in a future step.

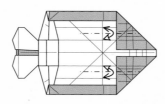

45 Mountain fold between the creases. This is a partial pre-crease that will be used for a collapse in a future step.

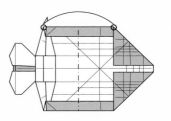

46 Fold edge to the crease from the layer underneath, letting the flap flip out.

Use crease from the layer underneath as a reference

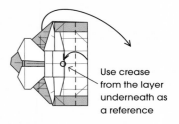

47 Pleat on the top layer. This will require a swivel under to make the model lie flat.

Start swivel from the folded edges in the inside

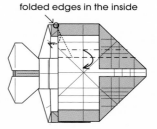

48 Swivel fold.

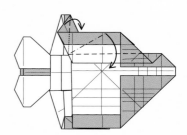

49 Fold edge to edge.

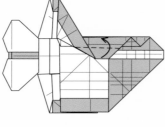

50 Repeat steps 47 to 49 on the other side.

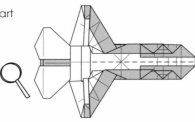

(47-49)

51 Fold the fuselage in half part way. Details of the cockpit next.

52 **a**

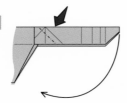

Inside reverse.

b

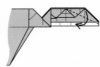

Crimp fold.

c

Valley fold on front and back.

53 Make the model 3-D: press to round the exhaust, then fold the wings up to shape them.

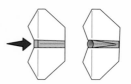

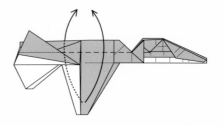

The completed fighter jet

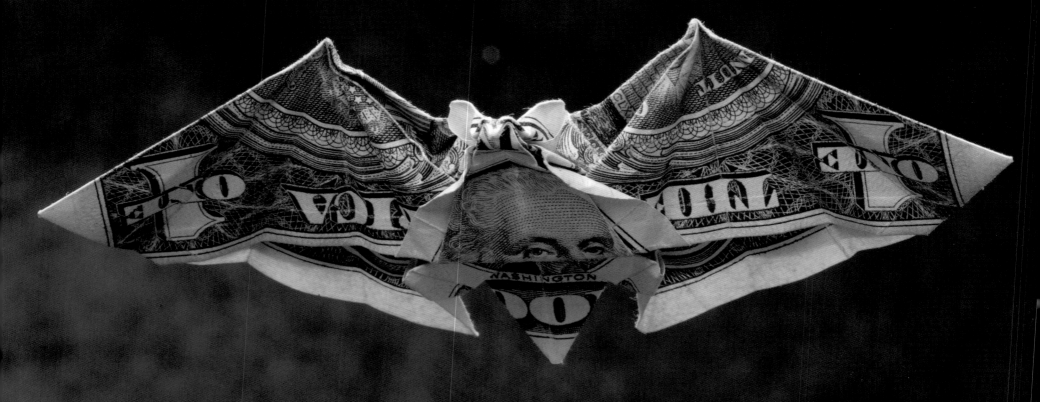

BAT

1 Fold and unfold.

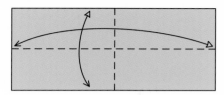

2 Fold and unfold top ¼.

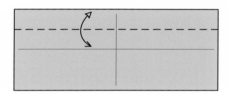

3 Fold and unfold the ⅛ and the ⅝ lines from the top.

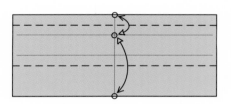

4 Mountain fold and unfold on both sides, aligning the first ⅛ horizontal crease line with the vertical center crease. The folds will intersect at the reference point.

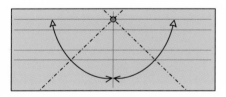

5 Fold and unfold parallel to the vertical center crease line on both sides. The vertical creases go through the intersection points shown.

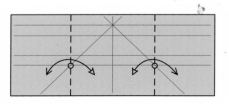

6 Mountain fold the ⅝ crease line to the vertical creases made in step 5. Unfold.

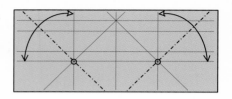

7 Mountain fold along the existing diagonal crease.

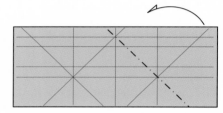

8 Mountain fold along the existing diagonal crease on the other side. Valley fold the flap to the side.

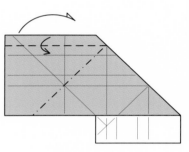

9 Turn over.

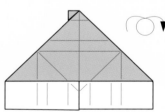

10 Use existing crease to flip one layer to the left. Squash the top.

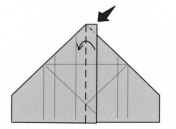

11 Fold on existing creases, squashing the left side.

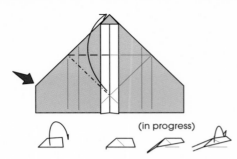

(in progress)

12 Open the model part way to allow the paper to flip to the back, reversing the valley crease to mountain.

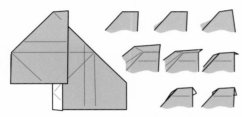

13 Fold on existing creases, squashing the bottom.

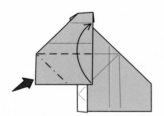

14 Repeat steps 11 to 13 on the right side.

(11-13)

15 Turn over.

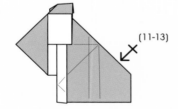

16 Valley fold the top layer only. You may have to move the flaps beneath out of the way. Unfold.

17 Fold the edges along the creases made in step 16 to create angle bisectors.

18 Using the creases made in the previous two steps, collapse the top layer into something resembling an upside-down bird base.

19 Fold the top flap down.

(Back view)

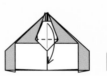

20 Pull out one layer of paper (indicated by the dots). The model will not lie flat.

21 Turn over.

22 Pull out one layer of paper (indicated by the dots). Move left and right flaps as far as they can go until the top edges are in line. At that point, the model will lie flat again.

(In progress)

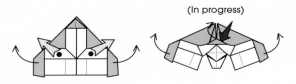

23 Turn over.

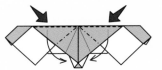

24 Inside reverse fold on both sides.

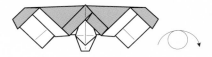

25 Inside reverse fold on both sides. Insert the flaps under the folded edges.

26 Turn over.

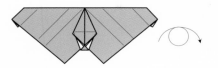

27 Fold the entire top flap down. You will have to open up the folds to allow the raw edge to switch sides and stay on the outside of the model.

28 Fold the raw edge out.

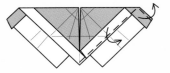

29 Valley fold the top layer only. Align the first crease parallel to the raw edge with the vertical center folded edge. Unfold.

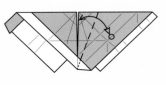

30 Mountain fold the top layer only from the reference point to the raw edge, forming a right angle.

(In progress)

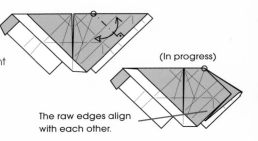

The raw edges align with each other.

31 Pre-crease for future step: mountain fold top layer only between the reference points. Unfold.

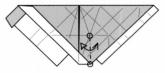

32 Pre-crease for future step: valley fold all layers, aligning the top edge with the crease formed in step 30, bisecting the angle. Unfold.

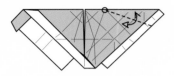

33 Pre-crease for future step: swivel using valley crease formed in previous step and the crease made in step 29. This creates a news mountain crease to flatten the model. See the next diagram.

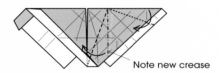

Note new crease

34 Flatten the model just enough to create the new mountain crease from step 33. Don't bother to flatten the bottom part. Unfold. Turn over.

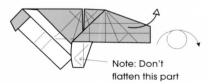

Note: Don't flatten this part

35 Mountain fold from the same reference point shown in step 32 (intersection of the diagonal crease with folded edge) to the reference point on the raw edge. Unfold. Turn over.

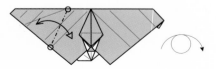

36 Squash using the creases created in steps 29, 30 and 35. See next picture.

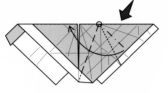

37 Repeat steps 29 to 36 on the left side. Next steps are shown in magnified view.

(29-36)

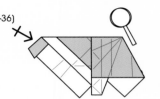

38 Use mountain crease created in step 31 to open right flap part way and form a wing. The model will not lie flat.

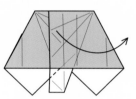

39 Create mountain crease on the top layer, using the folded edge beneath it as a guide.

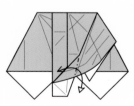

40 Valley fold along the vertical center line, squashing the bottom.

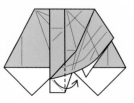

41 Repeat steps 38 to 40 on the other side.

(38-40)

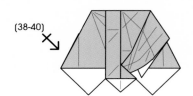

42 Fold what is going to become the head all the way to the top along the horizontal line of the bird base, and extend the crease to the left and right as you flatten until it intersects with the diagonal created in step 33. Unfold.

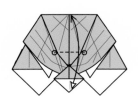

43 Open the wings and fold along the creases created in step 32 (the one from the back side).

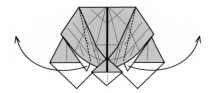

44 Flatten the head, neck and wings using existing creases. As you collapse, some new creases will form so the model will lie flat.

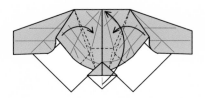

45 Move the top layer one layer beneath. No new creases will be formed.

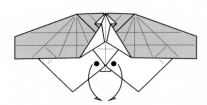

46 Open sink.

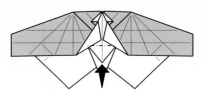

47 Move the flaps back to their original position in step 45.

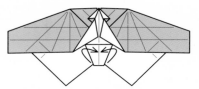

48 Tuck the corners inside the pockets beneath without making any new folds.

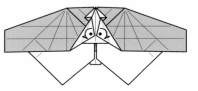

49 Mountain fold the top layer along the raw edge, then tuck it inside.

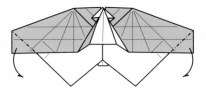

50 Mountain fold the top layer of the wings horizontally along what will become the neck of the bat.

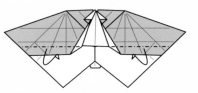

51 Fold the raw edges along the horizontal folded edge, bisecting the angle. Unfold.

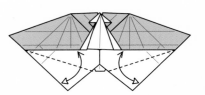

52 Fold the creases created in the last step along the horizontal folded edge, bisecting the angles.

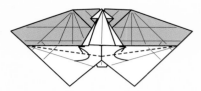

53 Valley fold.

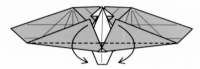

54 Valley fold the raw edges while squashing to flatten.

55 Mountain fold the raw edges, tucking them under.

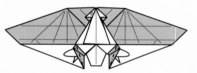

56 Valley fold the wing corners, tucking them inside.

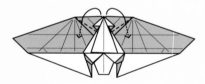

57 Turn over. Magnified views of the tail are next.

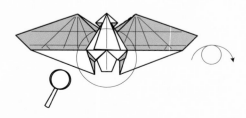

58 Start by swiveling the edges to the center vertical line. The model will not lie flat because of the extra paper.

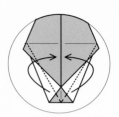

59 Fold the extra paper along the center vertical line. At this point, the raw edges should align with the folded edge. Create small crimps to flatten the model.

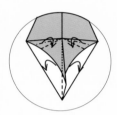

60 Fold the corners under.

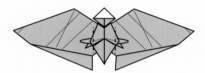

61 Mountain fold diagonally from top corner to the bottom corner of each wing. Unfold.

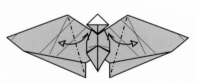

62 Mountain fold the upper edges of the wings to the creases made in the previous step, bisecting the angle. Unfold.

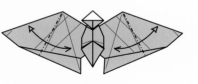

63 Create angle bisectors and unfold.

64 Add mountain folds shown to shape the wings and give them more dimension. Round the wings using the creases made in steps 61 to 63.

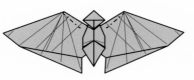

65 Next steps are magnified for details of the head.

66 Mountain fold the tip to create the bat's nose.

67 Valley fold from the corners of the nose to where the top folded edges overlap the layer beneath.

68 Valley fold horizontally to form the bat's face.

69 Open the ears. Use the tip of a pen or pencil or some tweezers to round the openings.

70 Turn over.

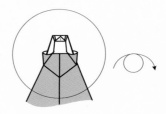

71 Rabbit-ear slightly to form the neck and give it some dimension.

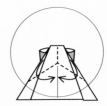

The completed bat

SCORPION

1 Fold in half. Unfold.

2 Fold the short edge to the long ones. Unfold. Turn over, flipping top to bottom. Valley fold on the intersection. Unfold.

3 Crease the angle bisectors by aligning the edges to the creases. Turn over.

4 Crease the angle bisectors by aligning the creases to the creases.

5 Collapse the waterbomb base.

6 Inside reverse fold the inner flaps using existing creases.

7 Pivoting from the intersection of the creases, fold point A and align the crease lines. Note that it will not reach the tip. No crease is created on this step, and the model will not lie flat.

A

8 Bring the flaps to meet, then press the areas indicated to flatten, making new creases. The inner layer should lie flat on existing creases.

(Area to be flattened)

(Area to be flattened)

9 Valley fold using the crease on the layer inside as a reference, so that the flap will stretch out and flatten completely.

10 Detailed view.

11 Make these creases for a rabbit-ear fold in the next step. After each crease, make the mirror image on the opposite flap.

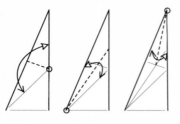

12 Rabbit-ear fold. Crease well. Unfold. Repeat on the other flap.

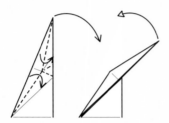

13 Valley fold the top layer to open up flap; press the center to flatten. Petal fold, then fold in half. Repeat sequence on other flap.

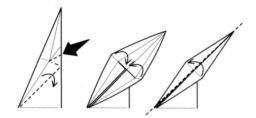

14 Create a small crimp fold inside so that the flap aligns with the edge. Repeat on the other flap.

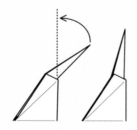

15 Turn over.

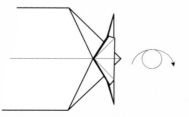

16 Fold the edges of the top layer to align with the center crease, from the tip to the folded edges hidden underneath. The model will not lie flat.

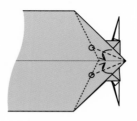

17 Release the layer that is trapped.

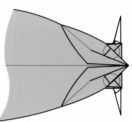

18 Swivel fold.

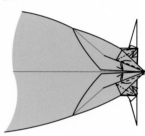

19 Shift the edges around the folded edges, allowing some paper to stretch to flatten.

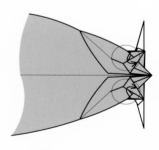

20 Turn over.

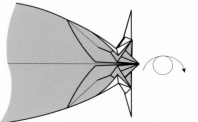

21 Start creasing along the edges from the sides. Crease to connect the references. Let the head fold over.

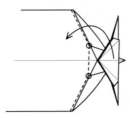

22 Flatten the area indicated. The model should lie flat.

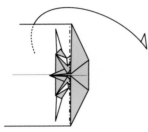

23 Fold the entire flap to the back.

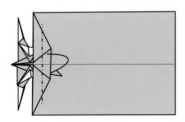

24 Mountain crease the folded edge.

25 Pleat. Start the first crease slightly bellow the edge, not on it.

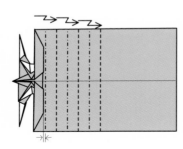

26 Detailed view of the pleats.

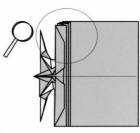

27 Inside reverse folding asymmetrically, starting from a point parallel to the center line, and ending in a point.

28 Continue reverse folding so that the edges becomes flush.

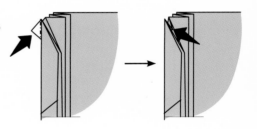

29 Repeat the inside reverse folds on the other pleats.

(27-28)
(27-28)

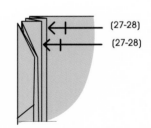

30 Repeat steps 27 to 29 on the other side.

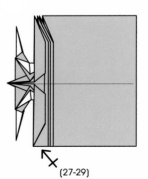

(27-29)

31 Pleat fold. The first mountain should align with the folded edge. The valley fold should leave the same gap used on step 26. Unfold. Turn over.

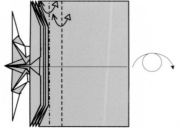

32 Fold the edges to the center line.

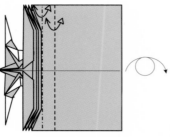

33 Fold the edges to the center crease, only to the first perpendicular crease. Unfold.

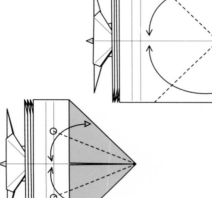

34 Pleat on existing creases.

35 Fold the edges to the center crease, allowing some of the paper to lift. The model will not lie flat.

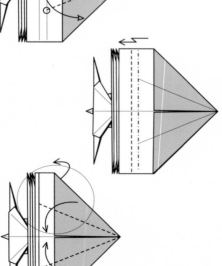

36 Press the area indicated, creating new creases to flatten.

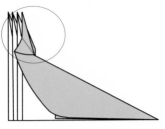

37 Fold upright to view the inside.

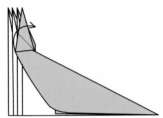

38 Push from back to pop up one layer, eliminating the edge on the front and defining the edges on this side.

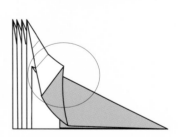

39 Press the area indicated, creating new creases to flatten. The model should lie flat now.

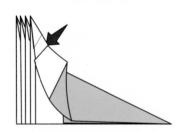

40 Fold from corner to corner.

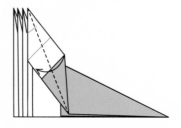

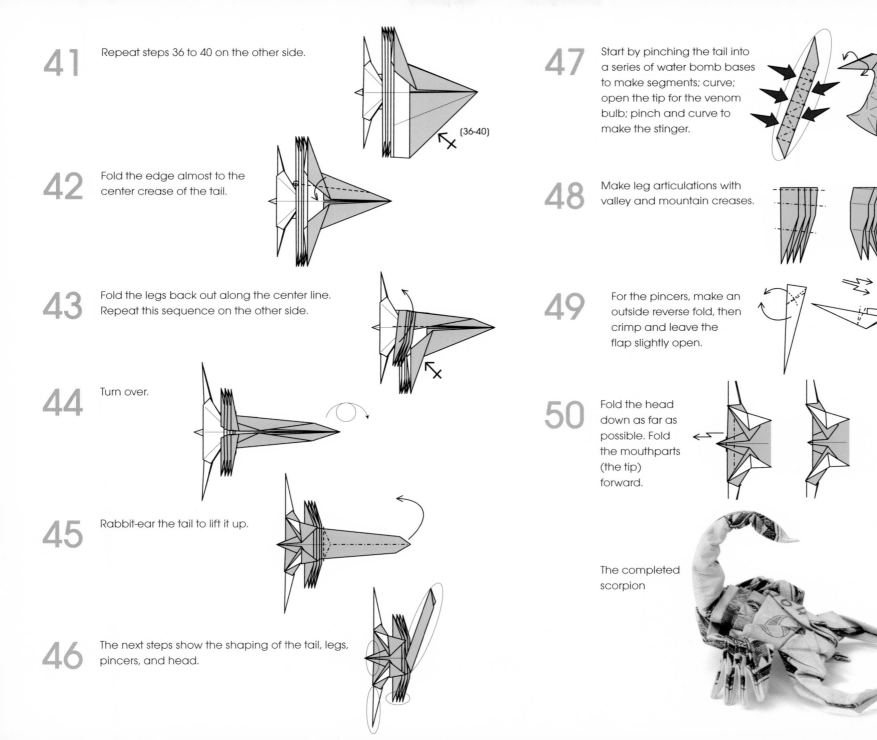

41 Repeat steps 36 to 40 on the other side.

(36-40)

42 Fold the edge almost to the center crease of the tail.

43 Fold the legs back out along the center line. Repeat this sequence on the other side.

44 Turn over.

45 Rabbit-ear the tail to lift it up.

46 The next steps show the shaping of the tail, legs, pincers, and head.

47 Start by pinching the tail into a series of water bomb bases to make segments; curve; open the tip for the venom bulb; pinch and curve to make the stinger.

48 Make leg articulations with valley and mountain creases.

49 For the pincers, make an outside reverse fold, then crimp and leave the flap slightly open.

50 Fold the head down as far as possible. Fold the mouthparts (the tip) forward.

The completed scorpion

KOI FISH

1 If using real money, start with the face side visible, but position the bill so George Washington is upside down. Fold in half lengthwise and unfold.

2 Fold the short edge to the long edges and crease only up to the central horizontal crease. Unfold.

3 Fold short edges to the central horizontal crease only up to the diagonals made in step 2. Unfold.

4 Fold vertically at the intersection of the creases. Unfold.

5 Pinch midway between the reference points.

6 Pinch midway between the reference points.

7 Valley fold midway between the reference points. Unfold.

8 Pleat using the creases, reversing the last crease from valley to mountain fold.

9 Mountain fold vertically along the folded edge. Unfold. Unfold the pleat back to the position in previous step.

10 Fold the edges to the central horizontal crease, creasing between the vertical edge and the pleat crease line.

11 Pre-crease for a future step. Mountain fold the raw edge along the diagonal, from the corner to the horizontal line.

12 Pre-crease for a future step. Mountain fold parallel to the diagonal created in step 3.

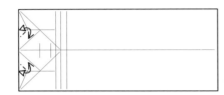

13 Fold short edge along the long edge.

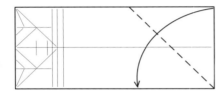

14 Fold the corner to the long edge and unfold. Unfold the flap made in step 13.

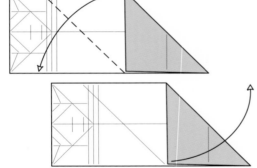

15 Repeat steps 13 and 14 on the other side, creating mirror-image creases.

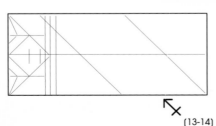

(13-14)

16 Fold and unfold.

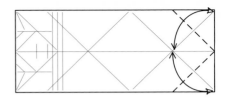

17 Fold in half (crease to crease).

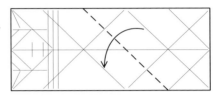

18 Fold edge to edge, unfold. Unfold the flap created in the previous step.

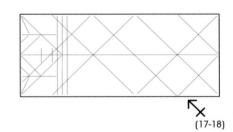

19 Repeat steps 17 and 18 on the other side, creating mirror-image creases.

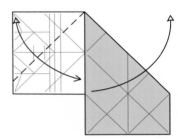

(17-18)

20 Fold between the lines, crease to crease. Unfold.

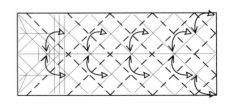

21 Fold between the lines once more, crease to crease. Unfold. Turn over.

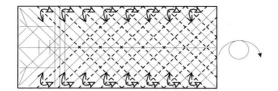

22 On the color (green) side, pleat using the existing creases (created in steps 7 to 9).

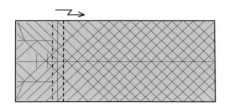

23 Find the small triangle immediately next to the folded edge, along the center. Using that triangle as a reference, mountain fold the crease that goes along its side. Unfold the pleat created in the previous step.

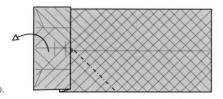

24 Extend the mountain crease started in the previous step. Mountain fold the next crease too.

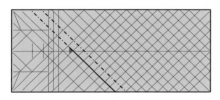

25 Bring the edges together creating a valley crease in the middle. Be as precise as possible and crease well.

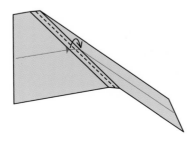

26 Unfold the long flap on the back.

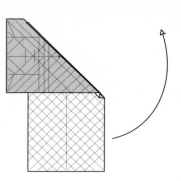

27 Valley fold using the next crease line. Turn over.

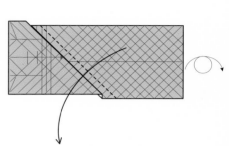

28 Bring folded edge to the crease line, allowing the flap to flip out from behind.

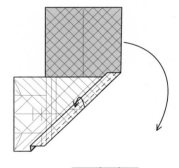

29 Turn over. Repeat the pleating process (steps 24 to 28) to the end of the dollar bill.

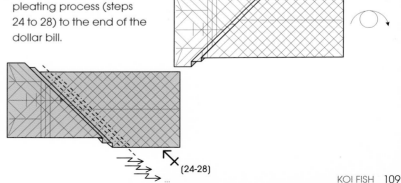

(24-28)

30 Unfold everything. Flatten the dollar bill as much as possible to crease the other side to avoid paper creep.

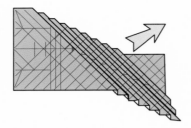

31 Narrow the gridlines going in the other direction using the same technique described in steps 24 to 30.

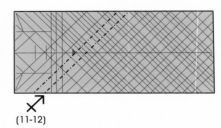

(11-12)

32 Pleat again, but this time alternating sides. Pleat one side, then the other (all layers) and so on. The result should be symmetrical.

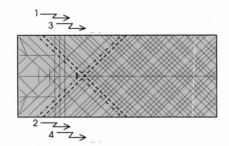

33 Locate the crease created in step 9. Valley fold the entire side, which will become the head of the koi fish. Crease well.

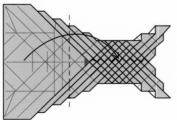

34 Turn over. Rotate 90° clockwise.

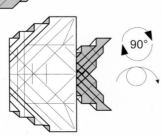

90°

35 Unpleat (pull the paper out) at the references. The model will not lie flat. Crease the folded edge.

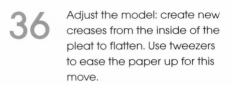

36 Adjust the model: create new creases from the inside of the pleat to flatten. Use tweezers to ease the paper up for this move.

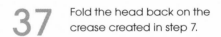

37 Fold the head back on the crease created in step 7.

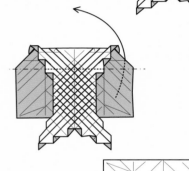

38 Pull the two pleats out and invert. The model will not lie flat.

39 Valley fold using the creases created in step 10, from the edge to the point where it intersects the folded edge on the back.

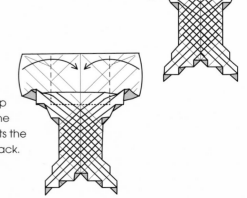

40 Pinch all layers together between fingers. The pectoral fins will not lie flat.

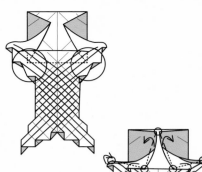

41 Start a crease from the folded edges up to the corners. Swivel fold until everything lies flat.

42 Rotate 90° counterclockwise.

(Detailed view of the fin viewed from the other side)

90°

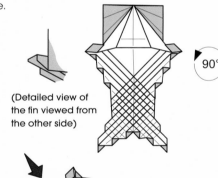

43 Inside reverse fold, using existing creases.

44 Inside reverse fold using creases created on steps 11 and 12. Note that on the underneath layer the raw edge will be perpendicular to the center line.

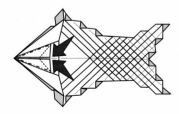

45 Fold in half gently.

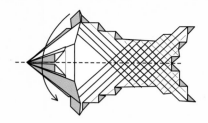

46 Crimp the head. Mountain fold on the folded edge on the back of the head. Valley fold between the reference points. Grasp the layers with tweezers along the guides shown and twist to mark the folds.

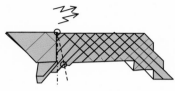

47 Lift the top layer to find the reference point. Notice that underneath, the head connects to the fin. Valley crease only up to that point. Don't crease further than that.

(Detailed view)

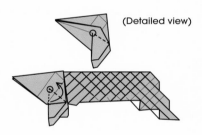

48 Start the crimp where the previous crease ended. Grasp the layer up to the reference point and twist to the right, using the edge of the tweezer to mark the crease. The printed pattern of the dollar bill should show, forming the eyes of the koi.

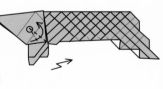

49 To lock, mountain fold between the reference points indicated (from the end of the crease on the top of the head to the corner of the fin). Repeat steps 47 and 48 on the other side. At this point the head should be tridimensional and will not lie flat.

(47-48)

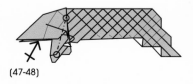

50 View from the top. Use the printed pattern as a reference; fold on line between the green and white. Make sure the fold is centered and crease well (use tweezers to pinch layers flat in 3-D areas).

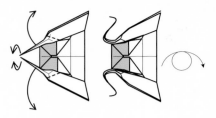

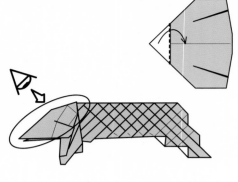

51 Use your judgment for this fold. Fold the tip forward, leaving a small edge, then fold the tip under. Crease well. Turn over to work on the whiskers from underneath.

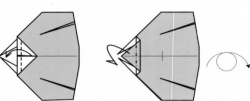

52 First, open the layers that might have gotten trapped during the crimping of the head. Flatten to make it smooth.

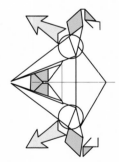

53 Rabbit-ear to thin the flap to make the whiskers. Use the tweezers to mark the folds, and then to pinch into shape.

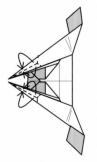

54 Move the whiskers so they point forward along the lips, and shape as desired by pinching and bending with tweezers. Turn over to the view from top.

55 Shape the lips with tweezers: first, mountain crease the center down. Then valley fold the corners back to lock.

56 Fold the pectoral fins out. Inserting a pen under the body, press the koi against it and round. Round the head, too, using tweezers to bend. Option: use tweezers to make little pinches to create a spiny back, which adds to the koi's beauty and realism.

57 To shape the tail, open the layers and look at the inside. Rotate for proper orientation.

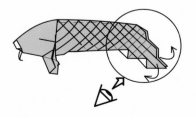

58 Pull out the first pleat, easing the paper from the center. Flatten, creating a new crease on the inside which will become the new folded edge.

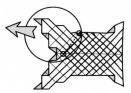

59 Fan out three pleats. Open and create a new crease inside to flatten.

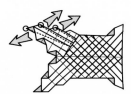

60 Fold back between the reference points, pushing out slightly to create a rounded edge. Crease well. Turn over. Gently fold in half.

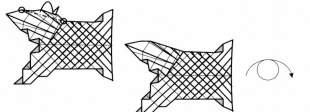

61 Fold up, from below the tip of the tail to the end of the second pleat.

62 Press tail back slightly, while rounding the back. Tuck the excess at the bottom inside, rounding the body. Make sure the tail stays up.

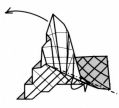

63 Curve the tip of the tail. Curl. Repeat steps 59 to 61 on the other fin, but position this fin down. Tuck the excess inside and curl as with the top fin. Finish shaping and rounding.

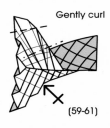

Gently curl

(59-61)

The completed koi fish

STEGOSAUR

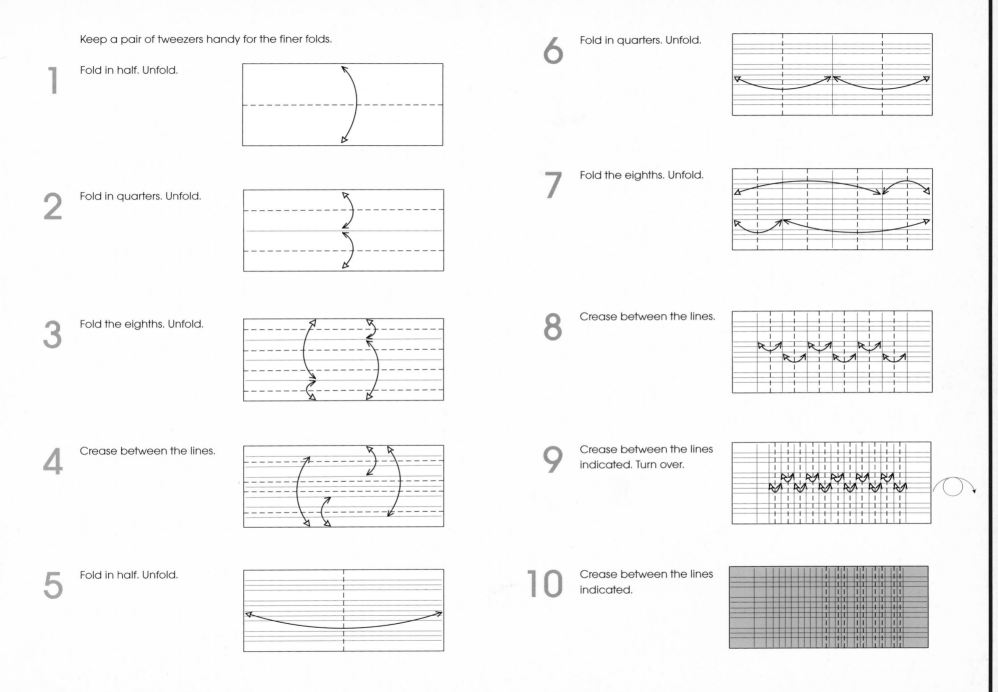

Keep a pair of tweezers handy for the finer folds.

1 Fold in half. Unfold.

2 Fold in quarters. Unfold.

3 Fold the eighths. Unfold.

4 Crease between the lines.

5 Fold in half. Unfold.

6 Fold in quarters. Unfold.

7 Fold the eighths. Unfold.

8 Crease between the lines.

9 Crease between the lines indicated. Turn over.

10 Crease between the lines indicated.

11 Fold edge to the center crease to form angle bisectors. Unfold.

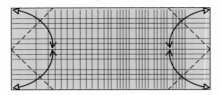

12 Fold edges to the creases. Unfold. Turn over.

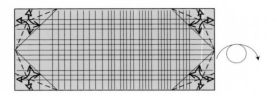

13 Fold the angle bisectors. Unfold.

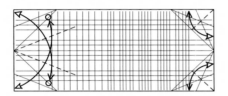

14 Fold the angle bisectors shown. Unfold. Turn over.

Crease all the way

Crease these to the intersection

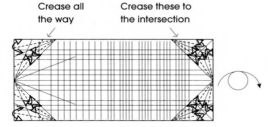

15 Detailed view of next step.

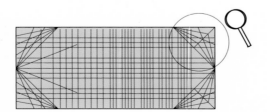

16 Start the collapse using the existing creases. The flap will not lie flat.

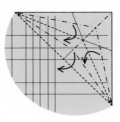

17 Push to create new creases and make the flap lie flat.

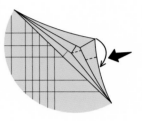

18 Repeat steps 16 and 17 on the other side.

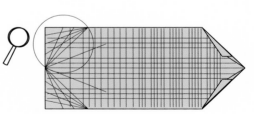

(16-17)

19 Detailed view of next step.

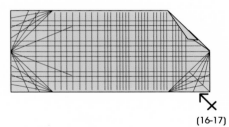

20 Pleat.

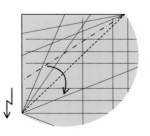

21 Inside reverse fold using one existing crease.

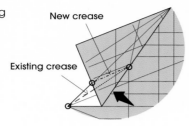

New crease

Existing crease

22 Pleat.

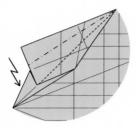

23 Inside reverse fold.

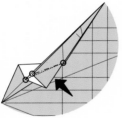

24 Form a sequence of inside reverse folds to make the edges flush.

Inside reverse twice

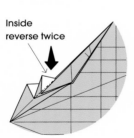

25 Form a sequence of inside reverse folds to make the edges flush.

Inside reverse four times

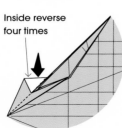

26 Result of the inside reverse folds.

27 Repeat steps 20 to 25 on the other side.

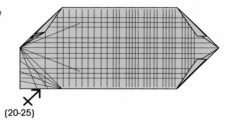

(20-25)

28 Pleat fold as shown to make the plates.

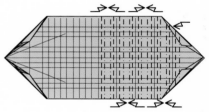

29 Pleat fold. Turn over.

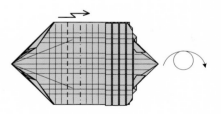

30 Swivel fold using existing diagonal creases.

New creases

Existing creases

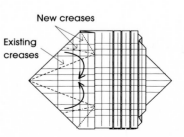

31 Valley fold on the existing creases.

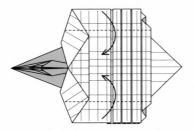

32 Valley fold to narrow the flaps.

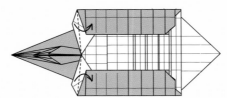

33 Valley fold through all layers between the reference points. Unfold.

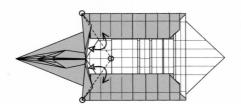

34 Mountain fold through all layers by aligning the edges to the creases. Start the creases from the edges up to the folded edges underneath. Unfold.

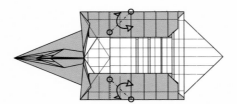

35 Mountain fold the layer underneath along the edge, between the reference points. Unfold.

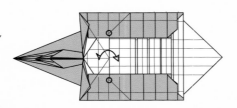

36 Mountain fold all layers between the reference points.

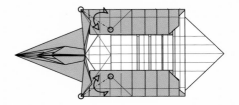

37 Valley fold the layer underneath between the reference points. Unfold.

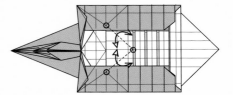

New creases

38 Lift part of the flaps using some existing creases and creating news ones between the points indicated. Model will not lie flat.

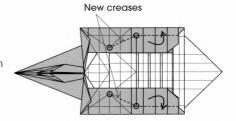

39 Fold in this order: (1) Mountain fold the tail in half before (2) collapsing the hind legs. (3) Then valley fold the bottom edge to the top edge.

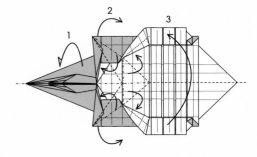

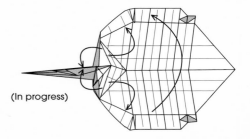

(In progress)

40 Push the bottom edge between the reference points in between the layers.

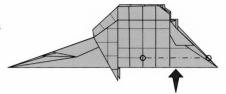

41 Push the top of the head down, squashing the layers to the sides.

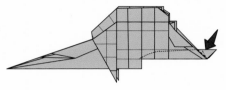

42 Release some of the paper trapped at the corner and then push, making a small inside reverse, and pull the flap down as far as it can go. This will form a front leg. Repeat on the other side.

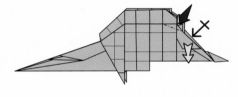

43 Crimp the bottom of the tail to narrow and give it some dimension. Pull the pairs of spikes up.

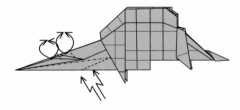

44 Details of the spine plates next. Helpful: use tweezers for the small folds.

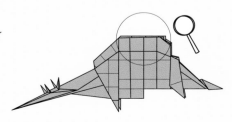

45 Shape the spine plates:

a

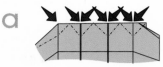

Inside reverse the small corners of the pleats.

b

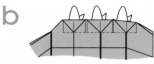

Fold the flaps inside.

c

View from the inside.

d

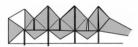

Inside reverse the flaps on the in-between layers.

e

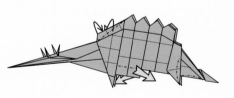

Sink the small waterbomb bases by partially opening them to rearrange the layers. Repeat steps a through e on the other side to make a second row of plates.

46 Final shaping details: tuck the excess paper along the spine to the inside, pull open the belly layers to create some dimension, then round the neck and front legs.

The completed stegosaur

DRAGON

You will need two pieces of paper for this model; one for the head and one for the body. Have tweezers at hand for the finer details.

Make the head:

1 Fold in half. Unfold.

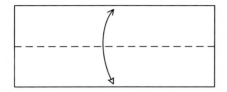

2 Fold in half. Unfold.

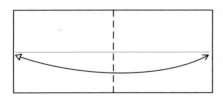

3 Fold angle bisectors by aligning short edge to long edges. Unfold.

4 Fold and unfold between the reference points.

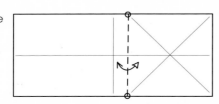

5 Fold edge along the center crease.

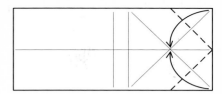

6 Fold edge along the edges. Unfold.

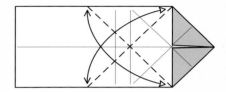

7 Fold edge along the edges.

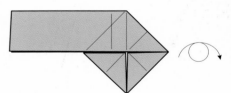

8 Turn over.

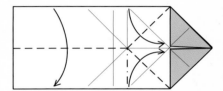

9 Fold in half. Unfold.

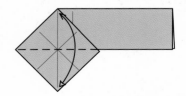

10 Fold the angle bisectors and unfold.

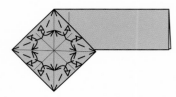

11 Collapse the preliminary fold.

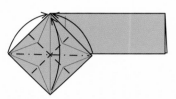

12 Collapse the bird base.

13 Open squash fold

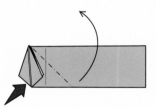

14 Inside reverse fold.

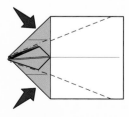

15 Open the model slightly to release some of the trapped paper, making an outside reverse fold.

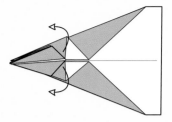

16 Inside reverse fold.

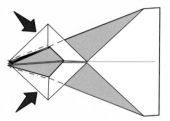

17 Open the model slightly and outside reverse fold.

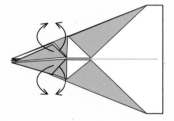

18 Swivel.

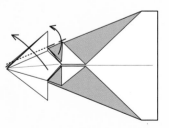

19 Fold one flap.

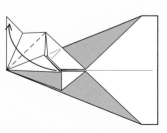

20 Fold one flap.

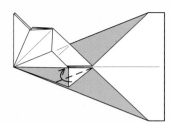

21 Fold flap, release the paper folded inside.

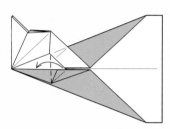

22 Fold the flap back and swivel back to the position in step 18.

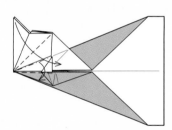

23 Repeat steps 18 to 22 on the other side.

(18-22)

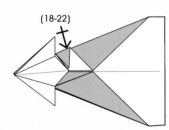

24 Open one flap.

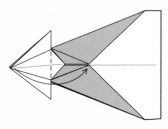

25 Fold as shown, then collapse into a preliminary fold.

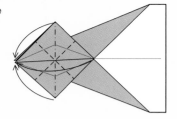

26 Inside reverse the four corners.

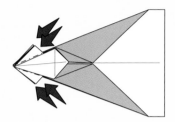

27 Fold in half, allowing the top layers to flip out to the other side.

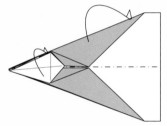

28 Pull out the paper folded inside.

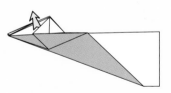

29 Fold the edge between the layers, then wrap the flap over the folded edge.

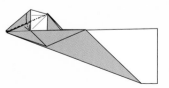

30 Unfold, bringing the model back to the position in step 27.

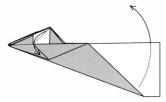

31 Repeat steps 27 to 30 on the other side.

(27-30)

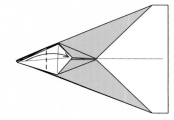

32 Fold the flap on the top.

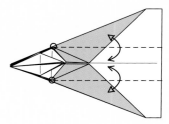

33 Fold parallel to the center starting from the reference points.

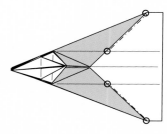

34 Crease along the folded edges between the reference points.

35 Crease between the reference points and fold the flap under. The model will not lie flat.

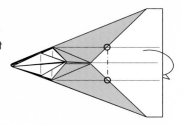

36 Flatten the model using existing creases and creating new ones.

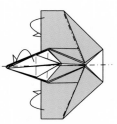

37 Inside reverse the layer at the bottom by creating new creases along the edge while folding the top in half.

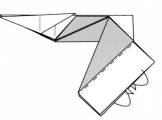

38 Inside reverse along the edge. If some paper does not fit completely inside, make a very small inside reverse inside to accommodate the excess paper.

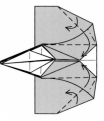

39 Details of the legs are next.

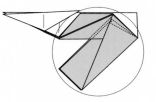

40 Make a series of mountain folds along the edges on both sides to form the points.

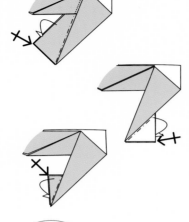

41 Details of the head are next.

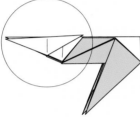

42

a

Outside reverse fold.

b

Rabbit-ear fold both sides to make horns.

43

a Inside reverse outside flaps to make teeth.

b Make a series of inside reverses on the inner flap to form the jaw.

c Fold ear flaps as shown.

44 Crimp the neck.

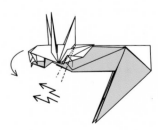

The completed head

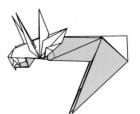

Make the body:

1 Fold in half. Unfold.

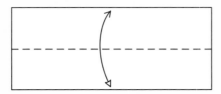

2 Fold in half. Unfold. Turn over.

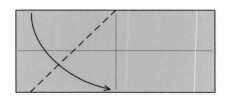

3 Fold the edge to the vertical crease.

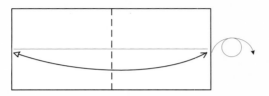

4 Fold the edge to the folded edge.

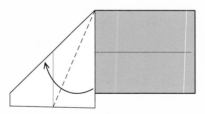

5 Unfold back to step 3.

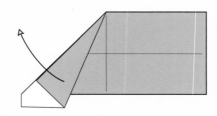

6 Repeat steps 3 to 5 on the other side.

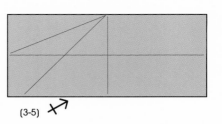

(3-5)

7 Mountain fold using existing crease.

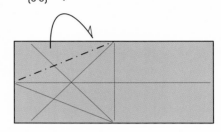

8 Use the existing crease to initiate a fold. Note that it will not lie flat.

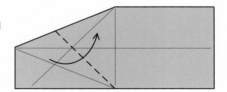

9 Align the edges and make news creases to flatten.

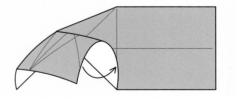

10 Unfold completely.

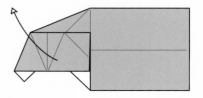

11 Repeat steps 7 to 9 on the opposite side.

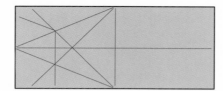

12 Fold the layer underneath in half, using existing creases. Do not make new creases on the top layers.

Do not form any new creases here.

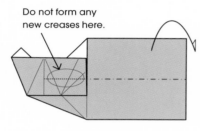

13 Fold using existing creases, allowing the top to flip over to the other side. Do not form any new creases.

Do not form any new creases here.

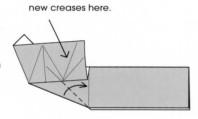

14 Turn over.

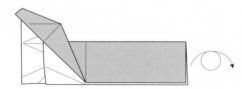

15 Using existing creases, open the layer so that it matches the one behind and the model becomes symmetrical, front and back.

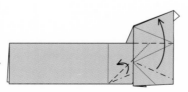

16 Create new mountain creases along the folded edge, then inside reverse. Rotate 45°.

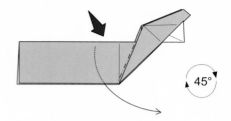

45°

17 Fold the folded edge to the raw edge, bisecting the angle. Unfold.

18 Inside reverse fold.

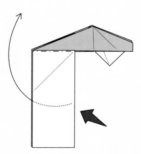

19 Inside reverse fold.

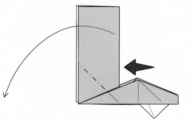

20 Pinch the half three times in a row to find the 1/8 reference.

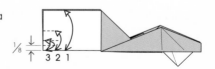

1/8   3 2 1

21 Valley fold from the ⅛ pinch to the intersection. Unfold. Repeat on the other side.

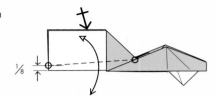

22 Inside reverse using the crease formed in step 21 and another made along the folded edge. Repeat on the other side.

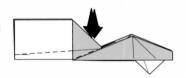

23 Inside reverse fold along the edge.

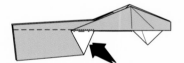

24 Inside reverse fold.

25 Fold along the folded edges.

26 Fold along the folded edges.

27 Fold along the folded edges.

28 Look inside, viewing from the top.

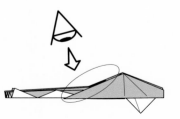

29 Create a mountain crease between the intersection of the creases.

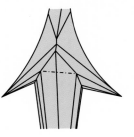

30 Create a valley fold crease, pushing the layers together and inward.

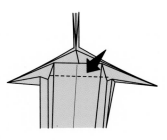

31 The model should lie flat now.

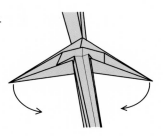

32 Fold the corner down as far as possible. Repeat on the other side.

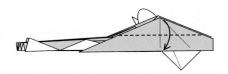

33 Inside reverse fold.

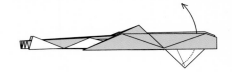

34 Inside reverse fold.

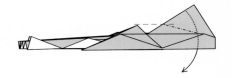

35 Inside reverse fold.

36 Inside reverse fold.

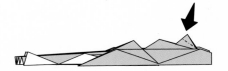

The completed body.

Assemble the head and body for final shaping:

1 Working on the head section, open the swivel fold. Repeat on the other side. Rotate 45°.

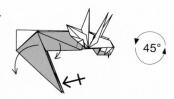

2 Insert the two flaps on the body section into the pockets on the head section. See next step for reference.

3 Swivel fold on existing creases, locking the pieces together. Repeat on the other side.

4 Use small clamps to train the paper.

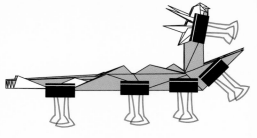

5 Details of the tail and talons next. Use tweezers here.

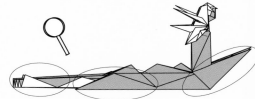

6 Shape the tail:

a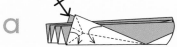

Rabbit-ear fold the outermost layer. Repeat on the other side.

b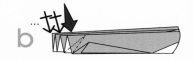

Inside reverse fold. Repeat on all flaps.

c

Inside reverse fold. Repeat on all flaps.

7 Shape the talons:

a

Valley fold through all layers. Unfold.

b

Mountain fold through all layers. Unfold.

c

Unfold the tip completely and spread it out.

d

Fold the tip under so that it fits between the folds like an accordion.

e

Inside reverse fold. Repeat on all flaps.

f

Inside reverse fold. Repeat on all flaps.

g

Pull out the tip to make the rear-facing claw.

h

Repeat steps a through g to make the remaining front and rear talons.

8 Shape the hind legs:

a

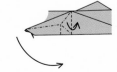

Rabbit-ear fold

b

9 Shape the forelegs:

a

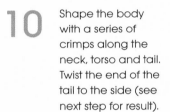

Rabbit-ear fold.

b

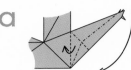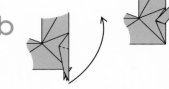

Valley fold.

10

Shape the body with a series of crimps along the neck, torso and tail. Twist the end of the tail to the side (see next step for result).

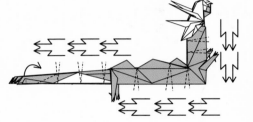

11

For final touches, curl the horns, shape the legs, and fan out the tail.

The completed dragon

DRAGON 131

FORMULA 1 RACE CAR

This model requires two units. Fold the same unit twice through step 18, then go on to make the modifications that will form separate front and back units. Have tweezers handy when making the wheels.

Fold two base grids:

1 Fold in half. Unfold.

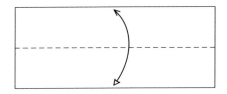

2 Fold in quarters. Unfold.

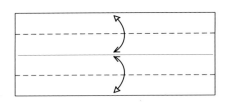

3 Fold the eighths. Unfold.

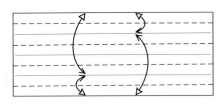

4 Crease between the lines.

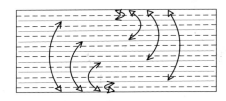

5 Fold the short edge along the long edges to make the angle bisectors. Unfold.

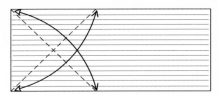

6 Valley fold between the reference points.

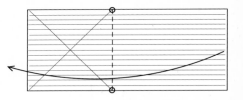

7 Valley fold, using the short edge on the back as a reference. Unfold.

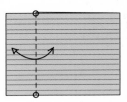

8 Unfold back to step 6.

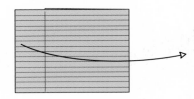

9 Crease between the lines.

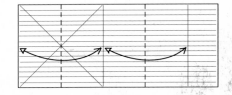

10 Crease the quarters between the lines.

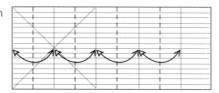

11 Crease the eighths between the lines.

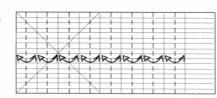

12 Crease between the lines.

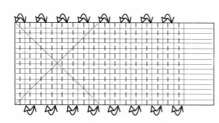

13 Valley fold on existing crease.

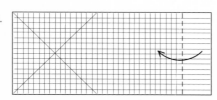

Fourth crease from edge

14 Valley fold using the crease underneath as a reference.

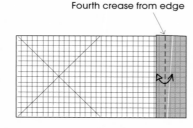

15 Unfold.

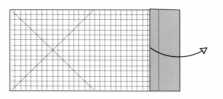

16 Crease between the lines.

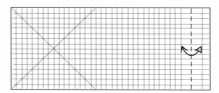

17 Crease between the lines.

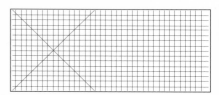

The completed base grid

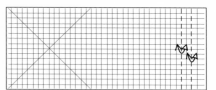

Form the front unit:

1 Start with a base grid.
Crease between the lines.
Next steps are magnified.

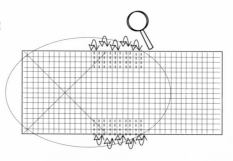

2 Crease the diagonals. Turn over.

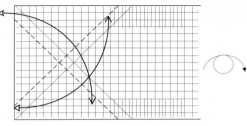

3 Fold the edges and pleat.

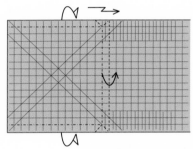

4 Collapse using the creases indicated.

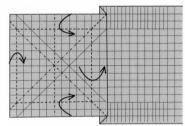

5 Collapse flat into something like a waterbomb base.

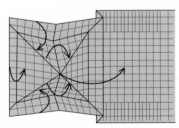

6 Open and squash.

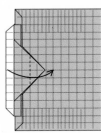

7 Valley fold the flap on the existing crease. This will require a squash on one side and a swivel on the other.

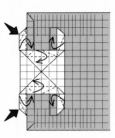

8 Outside reverse (you will need to open the model slightly to do this).

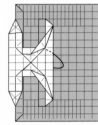

9 Fold the entire flap to the left.

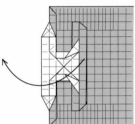

10 Fold the diagonals starting at the ninth crease from the left edge. Unfold.

Ninth crease from left edge

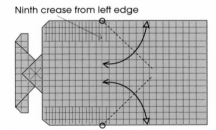

11 Mountain fold and pleat.

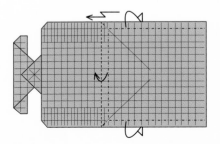

12 Collapse flat using the creases as indicated.

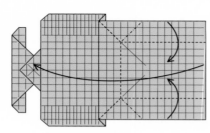

13 Squash and valley fold.

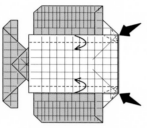

14 Valley fold.

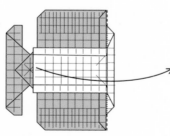

15 Fold the flap to the other side.

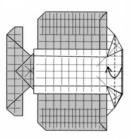

16 Valley fold.

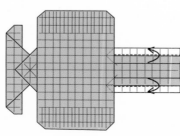

17 Pleat fold.

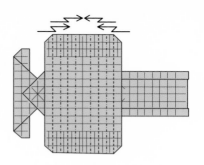

18 Form the cockpit: pleat and bring edges together as indicated. The model will not lie flat.

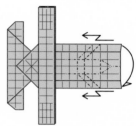

19 Pleat.

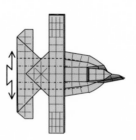

20 Inside reverse.

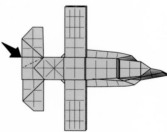

21 Fold the small triangular flap on the center line.

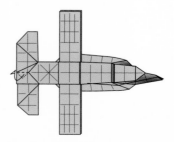

22 Repeat steps 19 and 20 on the other side.

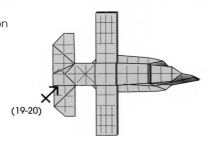

(19-20)

23 Detailed view of the seat from the side.

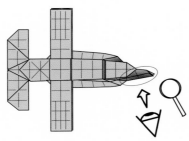

24 Shape the seat:

a

Inside reverse

b

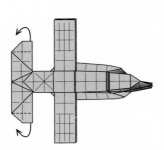

Valley fold the small triangle on both sides.

25 Shape the front wing by folding up the edges at an angle.

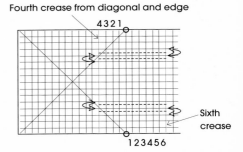

The front unit, ready for the wheels

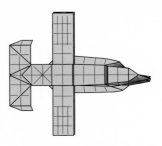

Fold the back unit:

1 Start with the other base grid. Valley fold on the last crease.

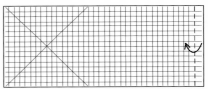

First crease from edge

2 Valley fold using the crease underneath as a reference.

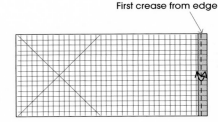

3 Unfold. The next steps are magnified.

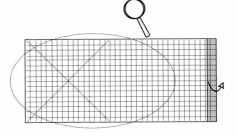

Fourth crease from diagonal and edge

4 Crease between the lines.

4321

Sixth crease

123456

5 Crease between the lines.

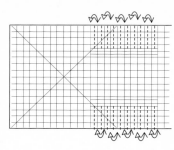

6 Crease the diagonals. Turn over.

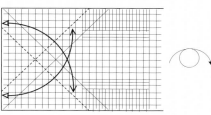

7 Fold the edges, then pleat twice. See magnified view next.

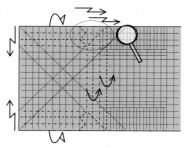

8 Collapse the waterbomb base.

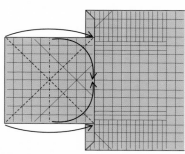

9 Open and squash.

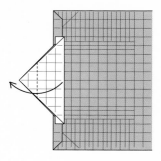

10 Valley fold.

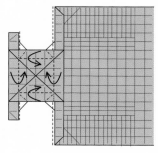

11 Fold the diagonals on the ninth crease from the left edge.

Ninth crease from left edge

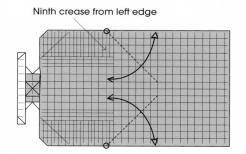

12 Mountain fold and pleat.

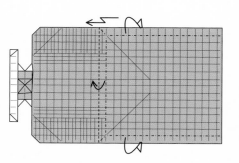

13 Pre-crease valley folds shown.

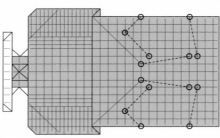

Create valley pre-creases.

14 Pre-crease valley folds and a set of mountain folds.

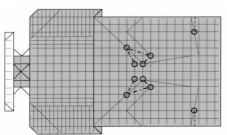

Create a valley and a set of mount precreases.

15 Mountain fold the narrow hem. Details of next steps are magnified.

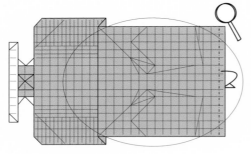

16 Start the collapse that will result in a small triangular shape (see final result in step 19). First, pleat as indicated. The model will not lie flat.

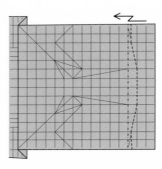

17 Continue the collapse in this order: (1) Flip out the long flap, then (2) Start the sink by pushing the sides as shown (some arrows are see-through so creases are visible).

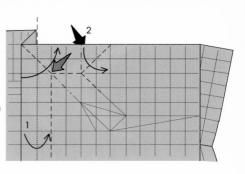

18 Finish the collapse: (1) Create a small pleat on both sides of the center crease, then (2) Push where indicated to sink both diagonals while pushing the sides inward so top edge will collapse flat. (3) Pinch the center so engine intake stands up.

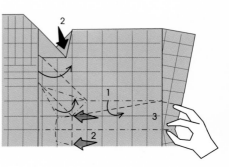

19 Pleat fold.

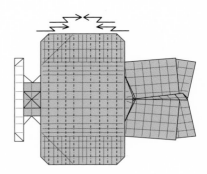

20 Pinch the center.

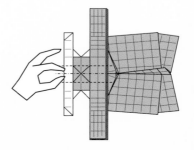

21 Rear wing details are magnified next.

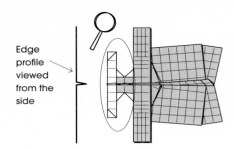

Edge profile viewed from the side

22 Form the rear wing:

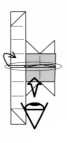

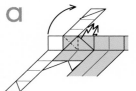

a

Crimp to fold perpendicularly.

b

Lift top layer only.

c

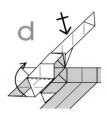

Push to allow edges to flatten.

d

Lift the flap vertically. Repeat steps a through d on the other side.

23 Engine intake details are magnified next.

Edge profile viewed from the side

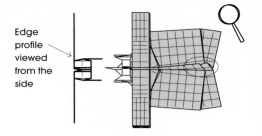

24 Inside reverse.

a

b

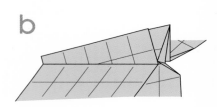

25 Mountain fold to shape the sides of the car's outer shell.

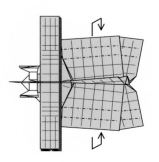

The back unit, ready for the wheels.

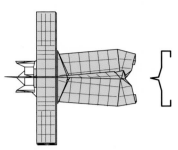

Final Assembly:

1 Form the wheels:

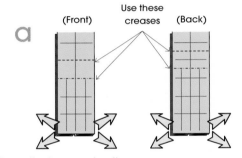

a

(Front)   Use these creases   (Back)

Open the layers using the creases indicated, then squash from inside to shape.

b

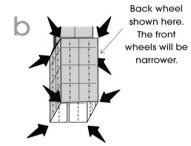

Back wheel shown here. The front wheels will be narrower.

Round further using existing creases.

c

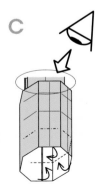

Fold the edge inside. Round edge around a pen or pencil.

d

(back view of the wheel)

Inside reverse fold by the axle. Helpful: use tweezers for the small folds.

2 Put the units together: insert the two small triangular flaps on the front unit into the pleat on the back unit to join the units together.

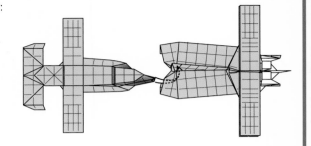

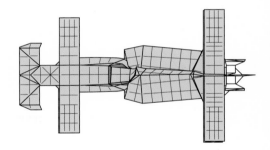

The completed formula 1 race car

ACKNOWLEDGMENTS

First and foremost, I would like to thank my parents, for without them I would not be here. I would like to thank my mother especially for introducing me to the art of origami. She was my very first teacher, one who showed me that a simple piece of paper can become a work of art.

To my high school art teacher, Debbie Tietgens, who was an inspiration to me when I did not know where I was going in life.
Thank you, Mrs. Tietgens.

I would also like to take this time to thank my guide through the world of book publishing, Nancy Hall, who has been there from the very beginning. From my very first public debut in OUSA in New York in 2002 to now, you have always stood by me and given me words of encouragement that I could do this. Thank you, Nancy, from the bottom of my heart. Thanks also go to Nancy's team, Tim Palin and Sherry Gerstein.

To my good friend and fellow origami enthusiast, Marcio Noguchi, who lovingly and painstakingly took the time to diagram my models, I cannot thank you enough for all the hard work you have done. I know that you have probably used my name as an expletive in times of frustration. I am very blessed to have you as a friend. Thank you.

To all my mentors that I have learned from though your books when I was a child (I spent many hours in my local libraries folding origami from their books): John Montroll, Robert Lang, Michael LaFosse who at first were my teachers that I only knew by name, I now have the honor and pleasure to call my friends. Also to countless other artists who have inspired me, and last but not least to the late, great Akira Yoshizawa—the father of modern origami. I want to thank you all for giving me the folding bug.

To Joel Bauer, who found me folding away in Hawaii and told me about the OUSA convention in New York and practically ordered me to attend. Just kidding, Joel! Thank you for showing me that there were other origami artists that were just as nuts about the art as I was.

To Michael Sanders, who has also been there from the very beginning. You have been my biggest advocate and a great friend, always there when I needed help and supporting my work. Also to Yukie and her family for being such gracious hosts and letting me stay in their home on my visits to L.A. You made me feel like family. Thank you both.

To everybody in my online Yahoo group, moneyfolders_unite, and my fans on Deviantart.com, thank you all for your support. It's for you guys that I make these books.

Hey, Andrew! You finally get to fold the $2 Dragon! Thanks for being so patient. You have always been one my greatest supporters and I thank you for that.

Also, a special thanks to Ron (tiny2th) my moderator for moneyfolders, thank you for all your dedicated work.

ABOUT THE AUTHOR

Won Park is an origami artist who been practicing the art for more than 30 years. His specialty is folding paper currency from the United States and other countries. Always striving to take the art form to new extremes, he has created a wide range of very intricate and whimsical models. He currently resides in Honolulu, Hawaii, with his fiancée.

For more information about Won Park and his models, contact him at *orudorumagi11@yahoo.com*.